THE SOARING
TWENTIES

BABE RUTH
AND THE
HOME-RUN DECADE

THOMAS GILBERT

THE AMERICAN GAME

FRANKLIN WATTS
A Division of Grolier Publishing
New York / London / Hong Kong / Sydney
Danbury, Connecticut

Photo credits ©: Transcendental Graphics: cover, pp. 84, 94, 119, 152; UPI/Bettmann: cover (bottom), pp. 15, 25, 53, 58, 88, 135, 141, 145; Bronx County Historical Society: p. 63; Chicago Historical Society: p. 40 (#SDN 62959—Chicago Daily News), 41 (#ICHi-19569); National Baseball Hall of Fame and Museum: pp. 7, 11, 21, 37, 73, 75, 99, 101, 116, 123, 126, 132, 146, 149; Photo File: p. 80.

Library of Congress Cataloging-in-Publication Data

Gilbert, Thomas W.
The soaring twenties: Babe Ruth and the home-run decade /
Thomas Gilbert.
p. cm. — (The American game)
Includes bibliographical references (p.   ) and index.
Summary: Discusses the changes in professional major league baseball during the 1920s, including the pennant race scandal in 1920, the founding of the Negro leagues, Babe Ruth's career, the farm system, and more.
ISBN 0-531-11279-9
1. Baseball—United States—History—20th century—Juvenile literature.
2. Ruth, Babe, 1895–1948—Juvenile literature. [1. Baseball—History.]
I. Title II. Series: Gilbert, Thomas W. American game.
GV863.A1G5756 1996
796.357'0973'0904—dc20
96-14464
CIP
AC

1 2 3 4 5 6 7 8 9 0 R 05 04 03 02 01 00 99 98 97 96

CONTENTS

CHAPTER ONE

*C*zar Search: The Beginning of the End of Ban Johnson

No two decades in baseball history were as different as the 1910s and the 1920s. Around the year 1920, the baseball world was turned upside down by one change after another. It all started with changes at the top.

Ever since Monopoly War IV ended in victory for the American League in 1903, Ban Johnson had been the uncrowned ruler of the major leagues. He was widely known as the "czar" of baseball. The peace treaty that ended Monopoly War IV—the 1903 National Agreement—had created a three-man National Commission, made up of the two league presidents and a neutral chairman, to govern the two major leagues. In practice, however, AL founder and league president Johnson controlled the commission chairman, Cincinnati Reds owner Garry Herrmann, and consequently held most of the cards. As the man who built their league from nothing and made many of them rich, Ban Johnson could count on the absolute loyalty of all eight original AL owners. As for the National League, whatever hard feelings its owners may have had toward Johnson were eased by the tremendous growth and prosperity of the baseball business during the dead-ball era. Johnson governed baseball with an iron hand, swiftly and surely punishing any owner or player who raised a dissenting voice.

Toward the end of the dead-ball era in the late 1910s, things began to change. Ban Johnson still played the part of a dictator, but his authority was rapidly diminishing. There were a lot of reasons for this, among them a series of political blunders by Johnson that divided the two leagues and alienated several long-time baseball owners. Once assets in his efforts to keep the fractious major-league owners in line, the ex-newspaper columnist's arrogance and combativeness were now playing into the hands of his enemies. Despite Johnson's lifelong obsession with the fight against gambling, there was a growing sense by the public that gambling-related corruption in baseball had never been worse. It was an open secret that first baseman Hal Chase and his band of merry game-throwers were fixing scores, games, and even pennant races with impunity. In September 1919, Chicago Cubs owner Albert Lasker, a national figure in the Republican Party but a baseball novice, dared to suggest that baseball was facing a crisis and needed "cleaning up." He proposed replacing the National Commission with a three-man body made up of prominent Americans from outside baseball who would weed out the Chases and restore public faith in the national pastime. Ban Johnson laughed off the idea of turning the management of baseball over to amateurs, but within a year Johnson would find himself humiliated and powerless and would see baseball governed by a Republican federal judge handpicked by Albert Lasker: Kenesaw Mountain Landis.

The beginning of Ban Johnson's sudden fall from power can be traced back to the George Sisler affair in 1916; this was the first of four National Commission

For nearly two decades, American League founder and league president Ban Johnson governed major-league baseball. He was ousted from his position on the National Commission in 1921.

decisions in disputes over players that weakened Johnson's grip on power in baseball. George Sisler was a slick-fielding, left-handed first baseman who played 15 years, mostly for the St. Louis Browns, during the

1910s and 1920s. A terrific hitter for average, Sisler hit over .400 twice and batted .340 lifetime; he was elected to the Hall of Fame in 1939. In 1911, at the age of 18, Sisler had signed a contract with a minor-league club in Akron, Ohio, but changed his mind and entered the University of Michigan, where he played baseball for coach Branch Rickey. Under the letter of baseball law, Akron retained its rights to Sisler indefinitely. The problem was that as Sisler's status as a pro prospect rose during his outstanding college career, his contract was sold to another minor-league club and then to the NL Pittsburgh Pirates. When Sisler graduated in 1915 and turned pro, Pirates owner Barney Dreyfuss maintained that Sisler was his property. This was disputed by Sisler, who explained that he had been a minor when he signed the Akron contract, that he did not understand baseball law or the contract at the time he signed, and that, because he had never played for any of the clubs that claimed ownership of his services, they had no moral right to prevent him from signing for the club of his choice. When Sisler chose to play for the Browns, who were managed by his old coach Branch Rickey, the Pirates filed a grievance with the National Commission. When Commission Chairman Herrmann ruled in favor of the Browns, Pirates owner Dreyfuss was outraged. His outrage only increased over the next few years, as Sisler developed into one of the top stars in baseball. Dreyfuss accused Herrmann and Ban Johnson of favoring the AL and began to campaign for their replacement.

Next came the Scott Perry matter. Perry was an obscure pitcher who was sold by minor-league Atlanta to the Boston Braves in 1917 on a trial basis: the Braves paid $500 down and agreed to pay a further $2,000 if Perry made the team. The deal was never completed because Perry jumped to an outlaw league after a few games with Boston; the Braves never paid the $2,000. In 1918, however, Atlanta resold Perry to Connie

Mack's Philadelphia Athletics. When Perry reported to Philadelphia and began to win games, Boston protested that Perry belonged to them. Because the dispute involved a minor-league club, two minor-league officials were allowed to vote on the matter, along with Ban Johnson and his two fellow National Commission members. This five-man group handed down a 3-2 decision in favor of Boston, but Johnson, who had voted with the minority, encouraged Connie Mack to challenge the decision in court. When the court enjoined Perry from playing for Boston, the NL owners were furious. They pointed out that they had accepted the Sisler decision, but now that an AL owner had lost one, Johnson encouraged him to sue. Before a compromise was eventually reached, the NL lost its league president, John Tener, and nearly followed through on a threat to cancel the 1918 World Series.

The 1918 World Series between the Boston Red Sox and the Chicago Cubs turned out to be a complete disaster for Johnson and Herrmann, who provoked the two teams to strike before the fifth game by arbitrarily reducing the players' share of the gate receipts. Even though the strike was settled in the end, game five was delayed for an hour while an obviously drunk Ban Johnson lectured the players about patriotism and the "wounded soldiers and sailors in the grandstand." Bad feelings lingered, and in the postseason a group of owners, including Boston Red Sox owner Harry Frazee, quietly felt out former U.S. president William Howard Taft about taking over as National Commission chairman. New NL president John Heydler later said, "our league went all out for the break-up of the old three-man commission after that players' strike in Boston."[1]

Finally, in 1919 two intra-American League disputes alienated a trio of key AL owners from Ban Johnson. The first quarrel was over effective spitball pitcher Jack

Quinn, who was claimed by both the Chicago White Sox and the New York Yankees. When Johnson awarded Quinn to the Yankees, he made an enemy of his friend and supporter of 25 years, White Sox owner Charles Comiskey. According to some friends of Comiskey, the Quinn case had been merely the last straw in a series of Johnson decisions that went against the White Sox owner. In an earlier incident, for example, after Johnson had vacationed at Comiskey's Wisconsin camp, Johnson sent Comiskey a basket of fish along with a note that he was suspending White Sox outfielder Danny Greene for three days. As the story goes, an angry Comiskey asked: "Does he think I can play that fish in left field?"

The second dispute was over the foul-tempered submarine pitcher Carl Mays, a two-time 20-game winner who in July 1919 walked out on the Red Sox in frustration over the lack of support he received from the inept Boston fielders and hitters. "I'm through with this ball club," he told manager Ed Barrow. "I'll never pitch another game for the Red Sox." Mays then went on a long fishing trip and several AL pennant contenders, including the Yankees, opened trade talks with Red Sox owner Harry Frazee for the talented pitcher. A deal was soon done: New York owners Jacob Ruppert and Tillinghast Huston landed Mays for $40,000 and two pitchers. When Ban Johnson heard the news, he became furious and suspended Mays indefinitely. His reasoning was that Boston should have suspended Mays for walking out on the team and that it was a terrible example to allow a player to profit—by moving to a winning team—from such a breach of discipline. "It was up to the owners of the Boston club to suspend Carl Mays for breaking his contract," Johnson thundered, "and when they failed to do so, it is my duty as head of the American League to act."

*In July 1919, right-hander Carl Mays
walked out on the Red Sox, who promptly
traded him to the New York Yankees.
Commissioner Johnson alienated the owners
of both teams by trying to negate the deal.*

The Yankees followed the precedent Johnson him-self had set in the Perry case by going before a judge and getting a court order that prevented Johnson or his umpires from interfering with Mays's contract with New York. On August 7, 1919, Mays made his debut in pin-stripes, beating the Browns, 8-2. After the season ended, Johnson made a characteristically petty attempt to get even with Ruppert and Huston, whose team had finished third. He ruled that Mays's eight Yankee victo-ries were invalid and therefore that Detroit deserved the third-place prize money for 1919. Teams received money bonuses for finishing first, second, or third, but not fourth.

As the 1920 season opened, the Carl Mays affair and its aftermath had split the major leagues into two bitterly opposed factions: the so-called "Loyal Five" of Johnson supporters—Frank Navin of Detroit, Connie Mack of Philadelphia, Jim Dunn of Cleveland, Clark Griffith of Washington, and Phil Ball of St. Louis (four of them original AL owners)—and 11 "Insurrectionists," consisting of Comiskey, new AL owners Frazee and Ruppert/Huston, and the eight NL clubs. His ally Charles Comiskey had turned against him, National Commission chairman Garry Herrmann had been forced to resign on January 8, and Ban Johnson—afraid that he would not be able to control a new commission chairman—was refusing to cooperate with NL president Heydler in the search for Herrmann's successor. Few could have suspected it yet, but in the summer of 1920 major-league baseball was about to face its darkest hour with no one in charge.

12

CHAPTER TWO

Death and the Lively Ball: The Black Sox Scandal and the 1920 Pennant Race

Unquestionably the most significant of the four National Commission disputes of the late 1910s was the Quinn case, because it caused Johnson to fall out with his old ally Charles Comiskey. And once you made an enemy of Ban Johnson, there was no turning back. From late 1919 through 1920 Johnson indulged in a bitter war of nerves against Comiskey; his goal was to ruin the White Sox franchise and drive Comiskey out of the game in disgrace. When the Black Sox scandal broke late in the 1920 season and threatened to put major-league baseball out of business by destroying the fans' faith in the game's honesty, baseball's chief executive—the National Commission chairman—was an empty chair and its de facto leader was distracted by a personal vendetta. This state of affairs was 100 percent the fault of Ban Johnson.

When you take a close look at the events of the 16-month period between September 1919 and January 1921, it is astonishing how swiftly Johnson paid for his sins. It also becomes clear that while baseball was outgrowing its czar of almost two decades, the game was also transforming itself on the field. In 1920 the action in baseball boardrooms, in front offices, and between the chalk lines interacted in fascinating ways. New York Yankees slugger Babe Ruth was taking advantage of new pitching rules that outlawed or limited use of the spitball, scuffball, and other "trick" pitches to transform the fundamentals of baseball batting. Thrilling the nation with his mounting home-run totals, Ruth introduced the major leagues to the long-ball dominated game of the future. During an August game between Ruth's Yankees and fellow pennant contender Cleveland, Indians shortstop Ray Chapman was accidentally killed by a high fastball thrown by Carl Mays, the pitcher that Ban Johnson had tried so hard to prevent the Yankees from acquiring in 1919. This incident led to another rules change that accelerated the home-run revolution even further in 1921. Meanwhile, the AL pennant race came down to a photo finish between Charles Comiskey's crooked White Sox, whom Johnson finally succeeded in crippling, in the final few weeks of the season, by forcing Comiskey to suspend most of the team's stars; Mays, Ruth, and the Yankees; and the resurgent Indians, sparked by Chapman's clutch-hitting replacement, a 21-year-old rookie named Joe Sewell. By opening day 1921, baseball was a new game under a new "czar" with powers beyond those even of Ban Johnson in his prime.

The final 16 months of the Ban Johnson era began on September 16, 1919, when the AL board of directors attacked Johnson publicly and stated that "the time has come when the powers of Mr. Johnson should be curtailed." According to the AL constitution, owners filled the directors' seats on a rotating basis. By the luck of the draw, the board happened to consist of Johnson's biggest enemies in baseball—Jacob Ruppert, Harry Frazee, and Charles Comiskey.

Charles Comiskey, owner of the Chicago White Sox, waits to testify before a Chicago grand jury in 1920 about the crooked 1919 World Series.

Less than three weeks later, on October 2, White Sox owner Comiskey was tossing and turning in bed, wrestling with a terrible problem. His team was losing the World Series to the underdog NL Cincinnati Reds, and his manager, Kid Gleason, had confessed that he feared some of his players were intentionally throwing the series. Comiskey wanted to alert a higher authority, but, as owner of the Reds, National Commission chairman Garry Herrmann was far from a neutral party; and after the September 16th announcement Comiskey and AL president Johnson were no longer on speaking terms. At 3 A.M. Comiskey decided to go to NL president John Heydler, who was staying at the same Cincinnati hotel; dressed in bathrobes and slippers, Heydler and Comiskey then walked down the hall to Johnson's room and woke him up. When Heydler told him why they were there, Johnson slammed the door in their faces, ridiculing Comiskey's suspicions as nothing but the "yelp of a beaten cur."

Shortly after the Reds polished off the series, five games to three, fans across the country began to hear rumors that gamblers had paid members of the White Sox to lose the series. Sportswriter Hugh Fullerton was one of the few who dared to put his suspicions in black and white. This sparked a backlash from the mainstream sporting press, including the *Sporting News,* which ran a blatantly anti-Semitic editorial blaming the rumors on "a lot of dirty, long-nosed, thick-lipped, and strong-smelling gamblers [who] got crossed [and peddled] stories that there was something wrong with the games." Deciding that there was no use crying over spilt milk, Comiskey tried a different tack: cover-up. He gave most of the suspected series-fixers raises in pay, threatened any guilty parties with the severest possible punishment—both measures designed to ensure the silence of any White Sox who knew anything about the fix—and proclaimed to the press that he would pay a $10,000 reward for any proof that the 1919 World Series was not on the level.

On November 19, 1919, the AL board of directors once again attacked Ban Johnson by claiming that his election as league president had been technically invalid. This time Johnson acted. He pushed through the election of a new board, provoking a flurry of suits and countersuits in New York courts. Characteristically, Johnson then went after each of the deposed board members in turn. He urged the New York Giants to evict Ruppert and Huston's Yankees from the Polo Grounds, where they had been a tenant. (The Yankees immediately began planning a new ballpark across the river in the Bronx.) He used a league investigation into gambling in Fenway Park to smear Boston owner Frazee. As for Comiskey, Johnson gathered evidence of the 1919 World Series fix and Comiskey's cover-up and bided his time; he intended to use this information against the White Sox owner when the time was right.

During the winter of 1919–20 utility infielder Lee Magee was released by the Chicago Cubs for throwing games. He sued for the balance of his two-year contract and threatened to reveal what he knew about "tricks turned" in baseball going back 15 years. Outraged that his fellow owners were more interested in hushing Magee up than in investigating his charges, Cubs owner Albert Lasker put out the so-called "Lasker Plan" to clean up baseball; it was met with little enthusiasm. The baseball rules committee outlawed the spitball and other "trick" pitches, but allowed 17 pitchers who relied mainly on the spitball to continue throwing it for the rest of their careers.

On January 8, 1920, Pirates owner Barney Dreyfuss finally collected Garry Herrmann's scalp. The Reds' owner, a close friend of Ban Johnson, was forced to resign, and Johnson agreed to cooperate with NL president Heydler in the search for a neutral successor, possibly a baseball outsider as called for in the Lasker Plan. Johnson rejected Heydler's first suggestion of Kenesaw Mountain Landis, a fiery Chicago federal judge who had aided the major leagues in Monopoly War V by delaying his ruling in the Federal League's antitrust suit. To Heydler's frustration, he soon realized that Johnson was determined to stall the search until some future time when Johnson would have regained enough power to dictate a choice.

Twelve days later theatrical promoter Harry Frazee shocked the city of Boston by selling phenom Babe Ruth to the New York Yankees for $100,000 plus a $300,000 loan. Frazee badly needed the cash to keep his show business ventures afloat. Red Sox fans were livid. "A Second Boston Massacre!" blared the headlines in Boston newspapers, referring to the 1916 sale of star center fielder Tris Speaker to Cleveland. Little did they know how badly they had been betrayed. In the years to come Frazee would choose to wreck the Boston franchise by paying off his Yankees loan with a steady stream of top-notch ballplayers, including catcher Wally Schang, outfielder Braggo Roth, shortstop Everett Scott, and pitcher Waite Hoyt. The fruit of the Babe Ruth deal would provide New York with the building blocks of one of the greatest dynasties in baseball history.

The AL owners met on February 10 to try to settle the dispute between Ruppert, Huston, and Ban Johnson. A compromise was negotiated on terms that were humiliating for baseball's former czar. The Yankees and Red Sox owners dropped all legal actions against Johnson, including the $500,000 damage suit filed by Ruppert and Huston on February 2. In return, Johnson agreed to reinstate Carl Mays and his 1919 victories, to give the Yankees their third-place money from that year, and, worst of all, to submit to a committee consisting of Ruppert and Washington's Clark Griffith that would review any large fines or suspensions handed down by Johnson. An interesting footnote to the compromise was that if Ruppert and Griffith could not come to an agreement, "a federal judge in Chicago" would cast the deciding vote. The skids were being greased for Ban Johnson and the way prepared for his successor.

On May 1, 1920, Babe Ruth hit his first homer as a New York Yankee; he went on to swat a dozen before the month was out. Ruth soon developed into a national sensation. Crowds packed AL ballparks screaming "crack it, Babe!" Observers marveled at the distinctive sound of Ruth's bat meeting a baseball; "it was like two billiard balls," wrote one sportswriter, "like a sound of solid things crashing together." On May 31, the Yankees set the all-time single-game attendance record by drawing 38,688 fans to the Polo Grounds. They would go on to fill 1,289,422 seats for the season and become the first team in major-league history to draw more than one million fans. For the sake of comparison, the Yankees had drawn 708,857 in 1919 and 256,618—*one fifth* of their 1920 total—in 1918. On June 15 Ruth tied his own single-season home-run record of 29, set with Boston the year before. Sportswriters searched for bizarre explanations for Ruth's home-run hitting ability. Some suggested that Ruth was a "physical freak" with superhuman strength; others speculated that the 1920 baseball had been manufactured differently in order to make it livelier. No explanation was offered, however, for the failure of the hundreds of AL hitters who did not hit 54 home runs to take advantage of the so-called "rabbit ball."

That same June in a Cincinnati federal court Lee Magee testified in his lawsuit for breach of contract against the Chicago Cubs. A utility infielder with nine years in the majors, Magee, who was born with the box score-busting name of Leopold Hoernschemeyer, had been released by the Cubs for fixing games. Magee had been caught red-handed but claimed that he had been led astray by the notorious Hal Chase when the two were teammates on the 1918 Reds. Needless to say, Magee lost the case. Chase had finally been kicked out of baseball late in 1919, after having cheated, fixed, and schemed his way through five teams over 15 seasons. He was now busy corrupting minor-league baseball in his home state of California. After a grand jury investigation into baseball corruption in Los Angeles, Chase was barred from setting foot in any Mission League park and became persona non grata in the Pacific Coast League as well.

By July and August 1920, the AL pennant race had come down to a nip-and-tuck three-team battle between Tris Speaker's Cleveland Indians, Babe Ruth's New York Yankees, and the chronically underachieving White Sox. In spite of the morale problems left over from the 1919 World Series disaster, the mysterious retirement of first baseman Chick Gandil—who was later discovered to have made at least $35,000, or almost *eight times* his yearly salary, on the Series fix— and a series of foul-smelling losses down the stretch, the White Sox were able to hang in the pennant race. As late as September 23 Chicago had four pitchers on a pace to win 20 games each and stood only a half game out of first place.

On August 16, 1920, Cleveland shortstop Ray Chapman, a respected team leader and one of the most popular men in baseball, was hit in the head by a pitch from Yankees pitcher Carl Mays. He died the next day, becoming the first and only major-leaguer ever to be killed by a pitch. Even though Mays had a reputation as a brush-back artist, there is no reason to suspect that he had intended to hurt Chapman; most eyewitnesses to the tragedy saw Chapman freeze on the pitch and some claimed that the 5'10" Chapman was crouching so deeply and crowding the plate so closely that Mays's pitch may actually have been a strike. Still, many inside and outside of baseball scapegoated the unpopular Mays for Chapman's death. Ban Johnson and his enemies found a way to bicker even about this. After

*Cleveland shortstop Ray Chapman died on
August 17, 1920, the day after he had his skull broken
by a pitch from the Yankees Carl Mays.*

Johnson publicly suggested that Mays might be better
off taking the rest of the season off, Charles Comiskey
laid the blame for the incident directly on Chapman's
inability to pick up the gray, beat-up baseball and indi-

rectly on Ban Johnson's policy directing umpires to keep discolored, worn baseballs in play to save money. Ruppert and Huston left Mays home on the team's next trip to Cleveland but backed their pitcher and vowed to continue using him for the rest of the season.

Babe Ruth belted his 43rd home run on August 19, the day before Chapman's funeral. Five days later, after the White Sox had swept the distracted Indians, Chicago was in first place, two games up on New York and three up on Cleveland.

A strange fluctuation in the betting odds on an August 31 game between the Philadelphia Phillies and the Chicago Cubs inspired widespread rumors that the game had been fixed. Over the next two days the White Sox dropped three straight to Boston and fell to second place, a half game behind Cleveland and a half game ahead of the Yankees.

After word of an internal Chicago Cubs investigation was leaked to the press, Judge Charles McDonald of Chicago convened a Cook County grand jury to look into charges that Cubs pitcher Claude Hendrix had conspired to throw the August 31 game. Within days, however, McDonald shifted the focus of the grand jury to the rumors surrounding the 1919 World Series. Ban Johnson welcomed the grand jury inquiry and claimed to reporters that he had heard the 1920 White Sox were still controlled by gamblers and that the team had been instructed to lose the pennant race to Cleveland. Years later, writer James T. Farrell recalled the scene at Comiskey Park on Sunday, September 26, after the White Sox had defeated Detroit, 8-1, to stay one-half game behind the first-place Indians. As the 19-year-old Farrell and a few hundred other young men and boys stood outside the ballpark, left fielder Joe Jackson and center fielder Happy Felsch—two of the eight Chicago players who, according to rumor, had conspired to throw the 1919 series—emerged from the clubhouse in their street clothes:

> *They turned and started to walk away. Spontaneously the crowd followed in a slow, disorderly manner . . . a fan called out: 'It ain't true, Joe.' The two suspected players did not turn back. They walked on slowly. The crowd took up the cry and more than once men and boys called out and repeated: 'It ain't true, Joe.' The call followed Jackson and Felsch as they walked all the way under the stands . . . and went for their parked cars. . . . Soon Felsch and Jackson drove by in their sportive roadsters, through the double file of silent fans. I went back to the clubhouse. But most of the players had gone. It was almost dark. I went home. I sensed it was true.*[1]

At about the same time, the Lasker Plan for replacing Ban Johnson's National Commission with one or more prominent outsiders was revived by the ad hoc committee to ban Ban, which now consisted of Cubs executive Bill Veeck, Sr., minority Cubs owner William Wrigley, principal Cubs owner Albert Lasker, Barney Dreyfuss, Giants owner Charles Stoneham, Harry Frazee, Jacob Ruppert, and Tillinghast Huston. President Taft, General John Pershing, General Leonard Wood, Senator Hiram Johnson, Treasury Secretary William McAdoo, and Judge Landis were among the distinguished, mostly Republican names floated by this group as potential leaders of a new baseball National Commission. "The mere presence of such men on the board," according to Lasker, "would assure the public that public interests would first be served, and that, therefore, as a natural consequence, all existing evils would disappear."[2] A number of AL owners objected to the plan's provision that the new commission or commissioner would have complete and unlimited power over managers, players, umpires, owners, and executives; he would even hold the power to ban any individual from baseball forever without any right of appeal.

The pace of events accelerated rapidly from late September on. On the 27th of that month, the first great tear appeared in the delicate fabric that had kept the 1919 World Series fix under wraps for almost a year. Under a headline reading "The Most Gigantic Sports Swindle in the History of America," *Philadelphia North American* sportswriter Jimmy Isaminger provided the first detailed look into the 1919 conspiracy. He interviewed a pair of small-time gamblers, ex-big-league pitcher Billy Maharg and Sleepy Bill Burns, who claimed that they had arranged financing for the series fix through another gambler named Abe Attell and that Attell had double-crossed both them and the eight White Sox players involved. Attell may or may not have been acting on behalf of his boss, the legendary bookmaker and underworld kingpin Arnold Rothstein. According to Maharg and Burns, the players had approached them, not vice versa, through pitcher Eddie Cicotte with an offer to throw the series for $100,000; in the end, however, the players received far less than that.

The next day Cicotte emerged from a meeting with Charles Comiskey, manager Kid Gleason, and club attorney Alfred Austrian and headed downtown to testify before Judge McDonald and his grand jury. Cicotte confirmed much of Isaminger's story, although he portrayed first baseman Chick Gandil as the ringleader of the plot. The 14-year veteran laid out the details of the fix and explained the art of throwing a baseball game. "It's easy," he said, "just a slight hesitation on the

24

Many people suspected that big-time gambler and mob boss Arnold Rothstein, pictured here in 1928, was behind the Black Sox scandal.

player's part will let a man get to base or make a run. I did it by not putting a thing on the ball. You could have read the trademark on it the way I lobbed it over the plate." On September 29, Joe Jackson testified and he too admitted guilt. Both told a similar story, that Gandil had been the ringleader, recruiting pitchers Cicotte and Lefty Williams, outfielders Happy Felsch and Joe Jackson, shortstop Swede Risberg, third baseman Buck Weaver, and utility man Fred McMullin and serving as go-between for the eight players and the gamblers. Both claimed that they had been double-crossed, with only Gandil getting the money he was promised. Comiskey promptly suspended the eight conspirators, telling each in a telegram, "If you are innocent, you, and each of you, will be reinstated; if you are guilty, you will be retired from organized baseball for the rest of your lives if I can accomplish it. Until there is a finality to this investigation, it is due to the public that I take this action even though it costs Chicago the pennant."

Sparked, ironically enough, by Ray Chapman's young replacement Joe Sewell, the Cleveland Indians won the AL flag by two games over Chicago and three games over New York. Sewell, who had batted only .289 in the minors, hit .329 with four doubles and 12 RBIs in his 22 games with Cleveland. The Yankees' Babe Ruth finished the season with an unthinkable 54 home runs, 25 more than the previous seasonal record and more than any other entire AL team. On October 12, Sewell and the Indians won the World Series, five games to two, over Wilbert Robinson's Brooklyn Robins. Rumors that this series was fixed were investigated by the Brooklyn District Attorney and found to be unsubstantiated.

THE YEAR: 1920

Sold by the Boston Red Sox to the New York Yankees in 1920, Babe Ruth played his first season as a full-time outfielder in the Polo Grounds. Blazing the way for a new wave of free-swinging home-run hitters, Ruth batted a Ty Cobb-like .376 but did so with extra-base hit totals the likes of which had not been seen since the

1860s. He lofted 54 home runs; the second-highest individual total was St. Louis Brown George Sisler's 19. Ruth led the AL in slugging at .847, to this day the highest mark ever recorded by a major-league hitter. AL pitchers knew when they were beat—they walked Ruth 148 times—but he still led the league in RBIs with 137.

Babe Ruth showed the kind of damage that could be done using the new, uppercut swing and other hitters soon followed his example. George Sisler, who in 1920 actually collected 11 more total bases than Ruth at 399, batted .407, the seventh-best average of all time, and banged out 257 hits, still a record. In the National League, slugging Cardinals second baseman Rogers Hornsby batted a league-leading .370 and led in doubles with 44, total bases with 329, and RBIs with 94.

After overcoming the accidental beaning death of shortstop Ray Chapman, the Cleveland Indians beat out both the Yankees and the White Sox in a tight pennant race. Ace pitcher Jim Bagby led the AL in wins with 31 and winning percentage with .721; teammate Stan Coveleski turned in an ERA of 2.49, second only to New York's Bob Shawkey at 2.45. The Indians met NL champion Brooklyn, who were led by Burleigh Grimes's 23 wins and 2.22 ERA, both third-best in the league; Cleveland won 5–2. On the Indians' side, the games were marked by several World Series firsts, including Elmer Smith's grand slam, pitcher Jim Bagby's homer, and Bill Wambsganss's incredible unassisted triple play.

On October 9 the NL owners voted to support the Lasker Plan and invited the AL owners to meet and discuss a new National Agreement on October 18. When the October 18 meeting was boycotted by Ban Johnson's "Loyal Five," the 11 owners who were present challenged the pro-Johnson forces to a game of chicken. They voted to dissolve major-league baseball as it had been known for 17 years, setting up a committee to devise a new structure along the lines of the Lasker Plan. They also gave the absent five clubs an ultimatum: if they did not sign on to the new plan by November 1, then the Insurrectionists would form their own league made up of their eleven clubs plus an expansion franchise in Detroit. This was shrewdly calculated to light a fire under Detroit Tigers owner Frank Navin, whose support for Johnson was thought to be wavering.

The "Loyal Five" showed some nerve in allowing the November 1 deadline to pass, but in the meantime Lasker and his allies were lining up support for Lasker's friend, Judge Kenesaw Mountain Landis, as the next commissioner; somehow the idea of a three-man commission seems to have been dropped. There was, however, still some fight left in the battered ex-czar. Ban Johnson fought the election of Landis tooth and nail. He demonstrated the breadth of his political influence when he persuaded Republican National Committee Chairman Will Hays to take time from his job running the Warren Harding presidential campaign—this was on November 1, only four days before Election Day—to lobby the Lasker group against the selection of Landis. On November 8 Johnson addressed a convention of minor-league clubs and delivered a powerful speech against the Lasker Plan.

Within a few days, however, the "Loyal Five" were beginning to fold their tents. Frightened at the potential financial cost of supporting Ban Johnson down the line, they sent Washington Senators owner Clark Griffith to open peace talks with Brooklyn's Charles Ebbets. On November 12 the 16 major-league owners met in Chicago without their league presidents. They agreed to a new two-league, 16-team structure under which the power of league presidents, Johnson included, was reduced almost to nothing. They also created an all-powerful National Commission chairman who would be the final authority on all interleague disputes and agreed to offer the job to Judge Landis. After making a group of owners wait for an hour or two in his chambers, like students sent to the principal's office, while he presided over a case, Landis accepted their offer of the baseball commissionership at an immense salary of $50,000, minus his $7,500 judge's salary, provided that he could remain on the federal bench. The owners granted Landis "absolute control" over baseball and gave him *carte blanche* to define his own powers and even to choose his own title. On January 12, 1921, the new National Agreement was signed and Landis formally installed as sole commissioner of baseball. The only consolation for Ban Johnson was the establishment of an advisory council made up of Landis and the two league presidents; only Commissioner Landis, however, had the right to convene this council and it was a right that he would choose to exercise only on the rarest occasions. The Lasker Plan was now in place, in effect over Ban Johnson's dead body.

Most baseball fans today believe that the baseball owners hired Kenesaw Mountain Landis to repair the damage done by the Black Sox scandal. They also believe that the 1919 World Series fix was a unique event, made possible by the chance coming together of several events: the low salaries paid to the White Sox by Charles Comiskey, the naiveté and gullibility of a group of unsophisticated, country-boy ballplayers, and the increased interest of gamblers in baseball caused by the closing of the racetracks during World War I. A close look at the events of September 1919 to January 1921, however, shows that at least one of these propositions is false.

There is no question that Ban Johnson's days were numbered well before the breaking of the Black Sox scandal. Even though the scandal helped create a sense of urgency among the owners about cleaning up baseball, dissatisfaction with Johnson and support for the Lasker Plan were both on the rise before Judge McDonald's grand jury ever met. The name Kenesaw Mountain Landis as well had been mentioned long before Jimmy Isaminger's exposé in the *Philadelphia North American* or Eddie Cicotte's confession. There is little doubt that Comiskey, Lasker, Dreyfuss, Frazee, Ruppert, Huston and the others would have succeeded in dumping Ban Johnson and installing Landis or someone like him with or without the Black Sox scandal.

As for the uniqueness of the 1919 World Series fix, this is also doubtful. It is true that no other series was ever proved to be crooked, but there have been rumors about the series of 1918, 1920, and others. And the conditions of the 1919 fix seem less unique the more you know about baseball in the dead-ball era. Far from being the unsophisticated dupes of dishonest gamblers and gangsters, the White Sox of the 1910s—and a substantial percentage of their contemporaries—were as hard-bitten, corrupt, and cynical a lot as ever played the game. Every believable account of the 1919 fix has the players approaching the gamblers with an offer to sell the series for cash, not vice versa. It is hard to believe that they had never done this kind of thing before. Many sportswriters and fans who followed the White Sox of the late 1910s were convinced that the team had been throwing games starting as far back as Hal Chase's stint with the team in 1913–14 and continued to do so through the 1920 pennant race. As for the rest of baseball, in his *Historical Baseball Abstract,* historian Bill James estimates that 38 major-league players were known to be involved in scandals between 1917 and 1927; 19 were banned outright or quietly forced to retire. Besides the eight Black Sox, they included such well-known players as Ty Cobb, Hal Chase, Rube Benton, Benny Kauff, Fred Merkle, Tris Speaker, Smokey Joe Wood, and Heinie Zimmerman. Undoubtedly, there are many scandals and many crooked players that will never be known. As the experience of Albert Lasker in the Lee Magee case shows, the owners of the time handled the problem of corruption and game-fixing by sweeping it under the rug whenever possible. Instead of disciplining or banning the Hal Chases of the world, they passed them from one team to another and covered up their misdeeds.

Why was the Black Sox scandal exposed when so many other potential scandals were covered up? An interesting argument could be made that the scandal served the interests of Ban Johnson and his allies among the owners in their fight against Comiskey and the Insurrectionists. Remember that during the 1919 World Series, Comiskey and NL president Heydler had gone to Johnson with their suspicions that the White Sox were throwing games. Even though there is independent evidence that Johnson already knew the series was crooked, he rejected Comiskey and accused him of making unsportsmanlike excuses for his team's failure. Shortly afterward, Comiskey took the familiar cover-up route. After all, the Insurrectionists did not need the scandal to topple Johnson; they already had him on the ropes.

Ban Johnson did take action in the Black Sox case, but he did so in secret. We know from Cubs secretary Harry Grabiner's journal, discovered by White Sox owner Bill Veeck in the 1960s and excerpted in his book, *The Hustler's Handbook,* and other evidence that Johnson hired private detectives to investigate the 1919 fix and Comiskey's subsequent cover-up. He then turned over what he had found to Charles McDonald, the Chicago judge who was presiding over the grand jury that ultimately indicted the eight Black Sox in 1920. Grabiner's journal is full of evidence that Johnson was secretly controlling the grand jury through McDonald—whom Johnson had promised the National

Commission chairman's job when the Lasker Plan, or something like it, went into effect—and that it was Johnson's unseen hand that changed the grand jury's focus from a single Cubs-Phillies game in August 1920 to the 1919 World Series. The idea was that Johnson would use the grand jury to create a scandal that would destroy the White Sox economically, expose Charles Comiskey as guilty of covering up the series fix, and cast McDonald as the savior of baseball. When McDonald was installed as National Commission chairman, Johnson would have another Garry Herrmann, a puppet through whom he could regain his one-man rule over the game.

The reason this did not work is that Ban Johnson fatally underestimated the political skills of Charles Comiskey, the son of Chicago ward politician Honest John Comiskey. Grabiner's journal tells how Comiskey planted a spy in Johnson's camp and followed his every move through the summer of 1920. Then, when McDonald's grand jury was at the point of breaking the scandal, Comiskey brought in Cicotte and the others himself, casting himself as the injured party—a betrayed boss who had only just discovered what happened in October 1919. When Comiskey suspended the eight Black Sox with two weeks to go in the pennant race he appeared to be taking the moral high ground, sacrificing a chance at the 1920 pennant for the good of the game. When the Black Sox scandal finally did break wide open, the tremendous public demand for reform advanced the agenda of the Insurrectionists and their call for an outside commissioner, not that of Ban Johnson and the status quo. The great irony of 1920 is that Ban Johnson, an implacable foe of gambling throughout his long baseball career, was swept out of power with the aid of a gambling scandal that would never have come to light without his great efforts.

A Commission of One:
Landis the Reformer

Fifty years after his death, Kenesaw Mountain Landis still casts a long shadow over the game of baseball. Other commissioners have come and gone, but none has come close to Landis in stature or power. Nearly every fan today knows Landis as the stern figure who cleaned up baseball after the Black Sox scandal and created the modern office of baseball commissioner. Many could identify him from a photograph. By contrast, very few would recognize the names of more than one or two of the seven men who succeeded him.

The son of a Civil War surgeon who served during General Sherman's infamous march to the sea, Landis was named for the Georgia battlefield where his father lost a leg to a Confederate cannonball, although Dr. Landis spelled the name of Kennesaw Mountain with only one "n." After Kenesaw Mountain Landis left his Indiana home for Chicago and a career in the law and in Illinois Republican politics, he was appointed to a federal district court judgeship by President Teddy Roosevelt in 1905. Landis resigned from the bench shortly after becoming the first sole baseball commissioner in 1921.

Like his predecessor Ban Johnson, Kenesaw Mountain Landis could be arrogant, arbitrary, and high-handed. Landis was also charming, fiercely honest, and dedicated to his personal vision of the greater good of the game. These qualities made him loyal friends and staunch enemies in the press and throughout the world of baseball. To historian Lee Allen, Landis was a hero who "made sure that what the spectators witnessed was as honest as the reflection from a mountain pool." To writer Robert Smith, he was a temperamental tyrant "possessed of a breathtaking egotism and a pathological urge to flaunt his power." Journalist Heywood Broun wrote wittily that Landis's career "typified the heights to which a dramatic talent may carry a man in America, if he only has the foresight not to go on the stage." However we judge Landis's character, the bottom line is undeniable: under his firm leadership the game of baseball cleaned itself up and became a revered national institution. His quarter century in office coincided with the time of the game's greatest stability and prestige. Fans who have lived in the post-Landis era can hardly imagine a time like the 1910s, when on-field corruption was rampant and a respectable businessman like Albert Lasker would hide his majority ownership in a baseball club behind a front man, (in this case, chewing-gum manufacturer William Wrigley), out of concern for his public image.

The owners did not mean to give Landis the power to do so much good. Proponents of the Lasker Plan had turned to Lasker because he was a prominent national figure with no financial stake in baseball; his only interest in the game was that he was a lifelong Cubs fan. To more cynical owners like Charles Comiskey, Landis's chief qualification for the job was that he could not be controlled by Ban Johnson, as Garry Herrmann had been. Few expected Landis to be a hands-on reformer; they thought that they were getting a figurehead who would provide the appearance of integrity without interfering with business as usual.

The cynics should have known better. Landis was an activist judge out of the reformist, trust-busting side of the Republican party. Never happier than when he was cracking down on important or wealthy wrong-doers, Landis used the federal bench as a pulpit for his political views, which were an unpredictable mix of anti-leftism, jingoism, and all-American rugged individualism. Landis disliked foreigners, organized crime, and big business. He believed in sticking up for the little guy and often gave extremely lenient sentences to defendants accused of crimes against large companies or institutions. On the other hand, he despised most organizations that professed to stick up for the little guy. His usual phrase for Socialists and union organizers was "those filthy, slimy rats."

Highlights of Landis's 15-year judicial career include his post-Armistice attempt to extradite German monarch Kaiser Wilhelm II to his court to stand trial for the murder of a Chicago man who went down with the *Lusitania,* a civilian ocean liner that was sunk by a German U-boat in 1916 before the United States had entered the war; his public brow-beating of millionaire John D. Rockefeller on the witness stand and subsequent $29 million antitrust judgment—the largest such fine in U.S. history up to that point—against Rockefeller's Standard Oil Company; and his sentencing of U.S. Congressman Victor Berger, an Austrian-born Socialist, to prison for opposing U.S. involvement in World War I. Both the Standard Oil judgment and the Berger sentence were reversed by higher courts on appeal. Cases like these illustrate that Landis was a judge out of the "To hell with the law; I know what's right" school of jurisprudence. They also earned him the nickname, "the most overturned judge in America."

Kenesaw Mountain Landis may not have been what the baseball owners wanted, but he turned out to be what they needed. A cartel, or monopoly, made up of members with drastically different interests operating in distinct markets, baseball at the beginning of the Landis era faced the same problems—poor labor relations, lack of economic balance, and squabbling among the owners—that it faces today. Of course, it also had a problem that modern baseball does not have: the selling of ballgames by crooked players. Landis was a shrewd politician who exploited this situation to maximize his personal power. During the winter of 1920–21, when he was negotiating with the owners, Landis held out for an almost unlimited mandate as commissioner. Though some owners complained that they were creating a new, even more uncontrollable czar, in January 1921 they caved in and begged him to accept the job on his own terms.

The first item on Landis's agenda as commissioner was to assert himself. Unlike many of his successors, Landis sincerely wished to speak and act for the good of the game; that included the interests of the fans and the players as well as those of the owners. This kind of independence required authority as great or greater than that of Ban Johnson at his peak. Ironically enough, it was Ban Johnson who helped Landis define his powers as broadly as possible. By challenging Landis's authority repeatedly in the first few years of his commissionership, when the baseball owners—still afraid of the lingering effects of the Black Sox scandal—would have given Landis anything to keep him from resigning, Ban Johnson provided Landis with the perfect opportunity to intrepret his powers as broadly as possible.

Johnson's first blunder was to repeat the mistakes of 1920. Determined to destroy his archenemy Comiskey and to be seen as the man who had saved baseball, he

36

*Kenesaw Mountain Landis became the first sole
commissioner of baseball in 1921.*

refused to let go of the Black Sox scandal. Sometime
during the winter of 1920–21 the confessions of Joe
Jackson, Eddie Cicotte, and the six other Black Sox mys-
teriously disappeared from the Cook County prosecutor's office. Some saw the hand, or wallet, of Arnold
Rothstein in this; others speculated that Comiskey could
have used his political influence to have the Cook

County prosecutor's office "lose" a few files. In any case, without the confessions criminal charges were dropped in February 1921, although the eight remained under indefinite suspension from baseball by Comiskey. Over the next few months and with the expiration date of the statute of limitations (a law that sets the time limit after the commission of a crime by which criminal charges must be filed) growing closer, Johnson became increasingly impatient waiting for Landis to pursue a new investigation and criminal prosecution of the 1919 series fix. Finally, when Landis told Johnson that the healthiest thing for baseball would be to let the matter rest, Johnson embarked on a two-month effort to rebuild the case against Jackson, Cicotte, Gandil, Weaver, Williams, Risberg, McMullin, and Felsch from scratch. Using his own personal funds Johnson hired detectives, traveled to Texas to interview witnesses and personally hunted down gambler Bill Burns and brought him back from Mexico. Armed with Johnson's new evidence, in July 1921 the Cook County district attorney brought the eight players and ten others, mostly small-time gamblers, to trial on the charge that they had engaged in a criminal conspiracy to defraud fans who had bet on Chicago to win.

Defense lawyers attacked the state's case on two fronts. First, they pointed out to the jury that even if the players did take money to fix the 1919 series—remember, the original confessions were lost and the players now maintained their innocence—this did not amount to a conspiracy to defraud bettors because the players would have been paid simply to lose games; whatever the gamblers might have done with their knowledge of the fix was not the players' responsibility. Second, they attacked Ban Johnson head-on, painting him as a vindictive deposed ruler, determined to get revenge on Charles Comiskey even if it meant letting bigger fish like Rothstein go free. "Ban Johnson was the directing genius of the prosecution," charged defense lawyer Michael Ahearn. "His hand runs like a scarlet thread through the whole prosecution. Johnson is boss. . . . He controlled the case. His money wired Burns and Maharg to dig up evidence. The State's attorneys have no more control over the prosecution than a bat boy has over the direction of a play in a World Series game."[1]

After being instructed by the judge that in order to convict, they would have to find that the ballplayers had intended to defraud bettors, not merely to throw baseball games, the jury took only a few hours to declare all eight players not guilty. In the courtroom, each verdict was met with wild cheering and throwing of paper confetti by the baseball fans who had crowded into the gallery, as if the White Sox had finally won the second and third World Series that might have been theirs had they been playing to win every game in 1919 and 1920. A gleeful Chick Gandil shouted: "I guess that'll learn Ban Johnson that he can't frame an honest bunch of ballplayers." Even the judge and the court officers waved and smiled at the victorious players, who capped off the evening by rendezvousing with the jury at an Italian restaurant, where they partied together until dawn.

If Ban Johnson was crushed by the verdict, he must have felt worse when he read the next morning's paper. There on the front page was the following ringing statement from Commissioner Landis:

Regardless of the verdict of juries, no player who throws a ballgame, no player that undertakes or promises to throw a ballgame, no player that sits in a conference with a bunch of crooked players and gamblers where the ways and means of throwing a game are discussed and does not promptly tell his club about it, will ever play professional baseball!"

39

*The Black Sox players (seated) pose with
their attorneys in a Chicago courtroom in 1921.
Although a jury found all eight players innocent of
conspiracy to defraud bettors, Commissioner Landis
banned them from baseball for life.*

Landis had banned the Black Sox from baseball for life, and he stuck by his decision. In spite of repeated moving pleas for reinstatement for Buck Weaver, Joe Jackson, and others over the years, Landis made sure that none of the Black Sox ever played another inning in organized baseball. In July 1921, Landis was hailed from coast to coast as a national hero. If it was true, as

Despite repeated pleas to be reinstated,
Joe Jackson never played a game in organized
baseball after the 1920 season.

many believed, that Landis supporter Charles Comiskey
had orchestrated a bogus acquittal for his players with
the idea of reinstating them for the 1922 season, then
Landis was an even bigger hero for having demonstrated his independence. By the simple act of making

permanent the eight players' suspensions, he had reha-
bilitated baseball and raised the game to a higher moral
plane than the criminal courts or the fan on the street,
the majority of whom—in Chicago, at least—told poll-
sters that they thought the players ought to be reinstated.

History has proved that Landis did the right thing for
baseball; the lifetime bans handed out to the Black Sox
sent out a strong signal to the rest of the major and
minor leagues that the rules had changed and there
would be no more tolerance for the Hal Chases and
Chick Gandils. Later in the 1921 season, Landis let the
owners know that the same rules applied to them when
he called Giants owner Charles Stoneham on the carpet
for having invited Arnold Rothstein, of all people, to sit
in his Polo Grounds box. Thanks to the Black Sox ban
and Landis's hard line on gambling, within a decade the
idea of throwing a major-league baseball game or fixing
a World Series for gamblers had become as unthinkable
as it is today. As for Ban Johnson, he was once again a
loser. He had spent months of effort and tens of thousands of dollars in dogged pursuit of justice in the Black
Sox case; and he had failed. Kenesaw Mountain Landis
had done nothing but give out a press release, yet he
was the savior of baseball.

Ban Johnson's first challenge to Landis's authority
was a typically underhanded and petty one. Johnson
had the language of the final draft of the 1921 National
Agreement altered to give the new commissioner the
power to "recommend" punitive action against players
or others who acted against the best interests of baseball, rather than to "take" such action, as the original
had read. When Landis spotted the change, he told the
owners to undo it or accept his resignation. "You have
told the world," Landis said, "that my powers are to be
absolute; I wouldn't take this job for all the gold in the
world unless I knew my hands were free." Needless to
say, the owners gave in. Again in 1923, Landis threat-

ened to quit if the owners objected to his taking away much of the league presidents' control over umpires and to his taking personal charge of the World Series.

From 1921 to 1926 Johnson and Landis had several run-ins, most of them calculated by Landis to remind the rest of the baseball world that Johnson was powerless to stop Landis from doing what he wished. In 1924 the two men feuded over a minor scandal involving the pennant-winning Giants. Based on a hasty investigation into allegations that a few Giants players had tried to bribe the Phillies to throw a game during the pennant race, Landis kicked New York outfielder Jimmy Connell and coach Cozy Dolan out of baseball but exonerated the rest of the team, including stars Frankie Frisch, George Kelly, and Ross Youngs. When Ban Johnson challenged the thoroughness of Landis's investigation and suggested that the World Series be postponed until the full extent of the corruption was uncovered, Landis was furious and refused to speak with Johnson or to send him his customary block of World Series tickets. When, after some grumbling and talk among the AL owners of trying to limit Landis's power, the AL owners told Landis that they wanted to end the stand-off, he insisted on unconditional surrender. The owners were forced to release a statement, dictated word-for-word by Landis, that reads in part:

> *We recognize that conditions have arisen that are gravely harmful to baseball and that must be intolerable to you [Landis] and that these conditions have been created by the activities of the President of the American League [Ban Johnson].*
>
> *While you were dealing promptly and efficiently with a most deplorable exception to baseball's honorable record, our President sought to discredit your action and to cast suspicion upon the 1924 World Series.*

43

One year ago you made known to us in his presence various of his activities and it was our expectation and hope that the unanimous action then taken certainly would operate as a recorrective, but in this expectation and hope we have been disappointed.[2]

It is hard to imagine how humiliating it must have been for Johnson to hear the owners of the AL, an organization that he had created from nothing, built into a great major league, and once ruled with an iron hand, publicly apologize for him as though he were an unruly child or a badly trained dog. In 1927, shortly after his last losing battle with Landis—a dispute over whether Ty Cobb and Tris Speaker were guilty of participating in a game fix; Landis exonerated and reinstated the two Hall of Famers after they had been quietly found guilty and forced to retire by Johnson—Ban Johnson agreed to resign from the AL presidency. A broken man, he died three years later of complications from diabetes. He was eulogized by *The Sporting News* as "the man whose reward for what he had done for baseball at large and his league in particular, has been a knifing that will be as historic as that handed Caesar."

THE YEAR: 1921

The home-run revolution spread across both leagues in 1921, as major-league home runs rose from 630 in 1920 to 937. Five whole teams batted over .300. Ruth hit 59 home runs for the first great team of the Yankees dynasty, making it three years in a row that he had set a new all-time record for most homers in a season. He led the AL in runs with 177 and total bases with 457, both the highest totals in history, as well as RBIs with 171 and walks with 144. Teammate Bob Meusel hit 24

44

home runs to tie Browns slugger Ken Williams for second place on the home-run list.

Not only did the New York pitching staff receive the best support in the league, 948 runs, it was first in team ERA at 3.79 and strikeouts with 481. Staff ace Carl Mays went 27–9 to lead the AL in wins and innings pitched; 21-year-old right-hander Waite Hoyt went 19–13 with a 3.09 ERA, fourth-best in the league behind Mays's 3.05. Tris Speaker's Indians failed to defend their AL championship by 4½ games; the 33-year-old Speaker hit .362 and led all hitters with 52 doubles. Sixth-place Detroit featured a strong hitting duo of young Harry Heilmann, who won the batting title at .394, and ageless Ty Cobb, who was second in hitting at .389, fifth in runs with 124, and third in slugging average behind Ruth and Heilmann.

New York Giants legend John McGraw won his seventh NL pennant behind strong performances from George Kelly, the NL home-run leader with 23; Frankie Frisch, who was first in stolen bases with 49 and second in runs with 121; and rising star Ross Youngs, who was third in RBIs with 102. New York beat off a strong challenge from a well-armed Pirates team that compiled the league's lowest ERA at 3.17 thanks to Babe Adams, runner-up in ERA at 2.64, and Whitey Glazner, third at 2.77. St. Louis Cardinals second baseman Rogers Hornsby took the batting title with a .397 average and led the NL in runs, hits, doubles, triples, total bases, RBIs, on-base average, and slugging average.

A year after baseball's partial ban of the spitball, pitching categories in both leagues were dominated by the 17 legal spitball practitioners. In the AL, Chicago's Red Faber led in ERA with a slick 2.48 and won 25 games, third-best in the league; St. Louis's Urban Shocker's wet one won 27. In the NL, the Cardinals Bill Doak soaked his way to the ERA title at 2.59 and led in winning percentage at .714; Brooklyn fans salivated at Burleigh Grimes's league-leading 22 wins.

The first-ever "Subway Series" proved that the new decade had changed the New York Giants' post-season luck. McGraw's NL champs came from two games down after two to win the 1921 World Series in eight games; they were helped by an injury that kept Babe Ruth out of the action in games seven and eight, which were won by the Giants 2-1 and 1-0. In the absence of the great Ruth pitching decided the outcome; Giants Jesse Barnes and Shufflin' Phil Douglas were the stars, going a combined 4–1; Waite Hoyt was the only pitching bright spot for the Yankees, compiling a 2–1 record on an ERA of 0.00. Ruth's wrecking crew were outhit, .269 to .207, and matched in team home runs by the Giants, 2-2.

After having marginalized American League president Ban Johnson, who had led the opposition to hiring Landis, and made a show of his independence from White Sox owner Charles Comiskey, Commissioner Landis set out to reshape baseball according to his own vision. "The opportunities for real service in baseball are limitless," Landis had announced upon taking office. "It is a matter to which I have been devoted for nearly 40 years. On the question of policy, all I have to say is this: the only thing in anybody's mind now is to make and keep baseball what the millions of fans throughout the United States want it to be." As much as this sounds like mere rhetoric, Landis meant it. Besides gaining virtually unlimited power to investigate and punish any action by any individual, team, or league, Landis insisted that baseball's new National Agreement make him the sole arbiter of disputes between the two major leagues and guarantee that there would be no diminution of his powers during his seven-year term of office. The new agreement also contained a promise

46

by the owners to refrain from challenging in court or even criticizing Landis's decisions, "even when [they] believe them mistaken." The famous trust-buster had become absolute boss of the most conspicuous monopoly in all of American business. "Such are the extraordinary prerogatives," editorialized *Baseball Magazine* in December 1921, "of a Czar, a Kaiser, and a Chinese Mandarin rolled into one which pertain to the simple name, commissioner, with which the owners have agreed to designate their new dictator."

At the time, there was no question that the commissioner's powers extended well beyond addressing the gambling problem. Landis's first act as commissioner was to settle a minor dispute between leagues over the player option rules. He was passionately involved in a variety of other business and labor issues, frequently acting as an advocate for the oppressed, underpaid, and union-less players against what he called—always making a sour face—"the baseball magnates." As part of what historian Lee Lowenfish has called Landis's "radical vision of a better baseball business," in late 1921 Landis proposed a universal draft—like the one we have today—distribute talent in a way that would be fair both to the owners and to the players. Later, in one of the few battles that he ever lost, Landis fought with the owners to try to stop the transformation of the independent minor leagues into farm systems in the 1920s and 1930s. He considered the death of the independent minors to be bad for the baseball business and unfair to individual players, who could be stockpiled in the minors indefinitely by big-league clubs. Twice he applied the drastic remedy of releasing nearly 100 minor leaguers from contracts with the Detroit Tigers and the St. Louis Cardinals. Throughout his reign Landis warned the owners that the reserve clause, which bound players to their teams whether they were under contract or not, was illegal. Later in life, Landis often indicated that if the players of the 1920s or 1930s had ever made a forceful protest against the reserve clause, he would have been delighted to rule in their favor.

Kenesaw Mountain Landis loved public attention and had an innate instinct for theater. With his permanent scowl and melodramatic shock of white hair he certainly looked the part of censor. As Bill Veeck once said, "if you lined up pictures of 100 men throwing out an opening game ball and asked a foreign visitor to pick out the man who looked most like a Lord High Commissioner, he would unhesitatingly point to Landis." By the force of his personality Landis promoted baseball as a quasi-patriotic institution and single-handedly transformed the World Series from a sometimes lackluster exhibition into the most prestigious event in the history of American sports.

Landis's influence was felt outside of sports. Inspired by Landis's success in reforming baseball, Hollywood film studio owners set up a commission to oversee the moral content of its movies and appointed another Indiana Republican politician, Will Hays, as a czar à la Landis to clean up their public image and stave off government regulation.

Commissioner Landis's tremendous public relations ability enabled him to foil periodic attempts by the unruly baseball owners to limit or diminish his powers. Not that they gave up trying. From the moment the crisis of 1920 and 1921 had passed, the baseball owners began to resent the authority of the commissioner. This was especially true when Landis turned his attention to them. As part of his campaign to rid baseball of gambling influences, Landis forced Giants owner Charles Stoneham and manager John McGraw to sell a race track, casino, and other valuable properties in Cuba. He banned Phillies owner William Cox for life for betting on his own team.

Long after the Black Sox scandal was forgotten and well into his second and third terms in office, Landis remained too popular to take on or fire. The owners, however, have gradually reduced the powers given his successors. Recent commissioners, enjoying what sportswriter Peter Gammons has termed "all of the power of the ambassadorship to Chad," have been little more than public-relations devices, exploiting the memory of Kenesaw Mountain Landis for what little influence they have been able to wield. They have been ignored and fired by the owners with regularity. Today the commissionership's governing functions have been stripped away. Its chief purpose has been to serve as a kind of scarecrow to keep Congress from removing baseball's antitrust exemption and imposing some kind of outside regulation on the game.

Landis's legacy of independence has been an inconvenience to the baseball owners of today. They have weakened the commissionership, but the owners have never dared to eliminate the office entirely. Today, years after they refused to hire a replacement for the last commissioner, Fay Vincent, the owners still refer to fellow-owner Bud Selig as the "acting commissioner." With collusion, the Pete Rose plea bargain, and the disastrous labor troubles of 1994 and 1995, baseball may well be returning to the chaos of the 1910s. The baseball commissionership stands as an imposing ruin, the relic of a time when Americans believed in moral authority and believed that baseball somehow embodied the nation's values. The power of Landis's memory is the reason why today's owners are simultaneously afraid to put another man in his chair and afraid not to.

CHAPTER FOUR

Long Gone: The Home Run and Modern Baseball

According to most baseball histories, in 1920 the major leagues adopted a livelier so-called "rabbit ball," Babe Ruth showed everyone how to hit it out of the park, and the dead-ball days were gone forever. The truth is that the change from pitching-dominated dead-ball to home-run oriented modern baseball was neither as simple nor as sudden as that.

To start with, no one has ever been able to prove that there was any significant change in the way the baseball was manufactured in 1920, 1919, or any other time thereabouts that suddenly made it livelier. In 1919 Ban Johnson made an off-the-cuff remark suggesting that the better quality Australian wool used in making baseballs after the end of World War I might have livened up the baseball. Baseball conspiracy theorists then and since have maintained that the major leagues slipped in a new, livelier baseball in or around 1920; explanations of the new baseball's behavior ranged from more tightly wound yarn to secret rubber cores.

50

The first problem with these theories is that all scientific evidence indicates that the baseball of 1920 was no different from that of 1917 or of 1924. In 1920 the Reach Company, which manufactured the baseballs for both major leagues, took out advertisements to proclaim that "there has been no change in the construction of the cork-centered ball since we introduced it in 1910." In 1926 *Popular Mechanics* magazine conducted an investigation into the ball controversy and concluded that there was zero evidence that the home-run explosion of the 1920s was caused by changes in the baseball. It also debunked the persistent notion among fans and sportswriters that the two leagues were using two different kinds of balls: a livelier ball in the AL and a deader one in the NL. There is one more good reason for doubting that the major leagues intentionally changed the way the baseball was made—they denied it. If it were true, there is absolutely no reason for major-league baseball to have lied about it. The baseball has been livened up, deadened, or otherwise changed many times in baseball history without any attempt to keep it a secret. In 1910 and 1911, for instance, the livelier cork-centered baseball was adopted openly. In 1926 the Reach Co. proudly announced the development of a new, livelier "cushioned-cork" centered baseball. As one sportswriter put it in 1921, "The manufacturers ought to know what they are talking about, and we can see no reason why they should deceive the public on this point."[1]

Second, there is no hard and fast line between where the dead-ball era ends and the home-run era begins. The two styles of baseball coexisted for many years. Babe Ruth's 54 home runs in 1920 may have shocked the baseball world and inspired a generation of young hitters to swing hard and uppercut the ball, but Ty Cobb and many other hitters continued to play dead-ball baseball well into the 1920s, slashing line drives and stealing bases as if it were 1905. Nothing shows better how these two baseball eras overlapped than the events of May 1, 1920.

Boston fans and Red Sox players alike had been horrified when their owner, Harry Frazee, sold slugging sensation Babe Ruth to the New York Yankees in 1919. But on Saturday afternoon, May 1, 1920, the fans who filled the Polo Grounds for the Yankees' game against Boston were wondering if they had really gotten such a good deal. Certainly, Ruth had turned the baseball world on its head in 1919, launching 29 home runs, a new record, in only 130 games. So far in 1920, however, Ruth was a huge disappointment; he had slumped through spring training, injured himself while striking out, and now—11 games into the regular season—he was still looking for his first official homer as a Yankee.

Some thought that it might be the ballpark. Even though Ruth had hit well during visits to New York the year before, the Polo Grounds was no hitters' paradise. Situated at Eighth Avenue and 157th Street in Manhattan, just across the Harlem River from present-day Yankee Stadium, the Polo Grounds featured unusually short foul lines. It was 277 feet from home plate to the left-field foul pole and a little over 256 feet to the right-field pole, but the outfield fence quickly bowed outward as it approached center field. The wall in the right-center power alley was an intimidating 449 feet from home and the left-center alley was even farther; dead center-field was somewhere around 485 feet away. Perhaps the most significant statistic about the Polo Grounds as a home-run park was that since its construction in 1911 only two men, Ruth twice in 1919 and the White Sox' Joe Jackson once in 1915, had ever hit a fair ball over the Polo Grounds grandstand.

As it turned out, Ruth was to choose this May 1 game against his former club, the Boston Red Sox, to break out of his slump in a big way. In addition to an

Red Sox owner Harry Frazee, perhaps the most reviled person in Boston's illustrious sports history, sold Babe Ruth to the Yankees in 1919.

RBI double, Ruth launched a massive home run off ace lefty Herb Pennock that took the fans' collective breath away: it cleared the right-field roof by plenty and landed in the infield of an amateur game being played on a nearby sandlot. The Yankees won the game, 6-0.

Ruth's May Day clout seemed to open the floodgates. He hit 11 more home runs in May and another 12 in June, both records. Amazingly, each of Ruth's first 16 home-park home runs of 1920 either reached the second deck of the Polo Grounds grandstand or cleared the roof.

By smashing one ferocious drive after another into distant parts of the ballpark that rarely saw action, Babe Ruth was beginning to alter the scale on which baseball was played. In early May the Yankees grounds crew decided that they had better paint the foul line on the outfield fences; by early June they found it necessary to extend the height of the foul poles from 15 or 20 feet to the top of the second deck, the normal height of foul poles today. Some people had trouble believing what they were seeing. *Baseball Magazine* printed a piece written by sportswriter F. C. Lane in early 1920 in which he doubted "the probability that [Ruth] would ever again make 29 home runs in a single season." By the time Lane's opinion reached the magazine's readers on July 1, however, Ruth had 24 home runs; in the end he surpassed his record of 1919 with 25 home runs to spare. Inspired by Babe Ruth, the rest of the Yankees hit 15 home runs in June and went on to swat 61 for the season; the 1920 Yankees' team total of 115 home runs was, needless to say, a major-league record. The home run revolution was in full swing.

If 1920 was the Year of the Home Run, however, somebody must have forgotten to tell the Boston Braves and the Brooklyn Robins. Two hundred miles northeast of the Polo Grounds at Boston's Braves Field on that same Saturday afternoon, May 1, playing with the same Reach baseball, these two teams played the single deadest dead-ball game in baseball history: a 26-inning 1-1 tie. To this day, this remains the all-time record for the most innings in a single game. Its length, however, is only one of many oddities from this artifact of a bygone baseball era. The absurdly low score is the first clue that these two teams were not playing baseball as we know it. Today, a poor hitter who goes 0-4 is mocked for having taken an "oh-fer" or "the collar"; it is even bigger news if a big leaguer goes 0-6 or 0-7, even in extra-innings. Yet in the May 1 game between Boston and Brooklyn two players went 0-10, and Boston second baseman Charlie Pick took an 0-11.

Then there is the amount of time it took them to play 26 innings: "From three o'clock until near seven in the evening" led the *Boston Post* the next day as it gave its readers the shocking news that the Braves game had lasted three hours and 50 minutes. Today, it is not unusual for nine innings to take that long. How did Brooklyn and Boston average under five minutes per half-inning? First of all, in true dead-ball fashion, the pitchers were throwing strikes; in the course of 26 innings the two teams totaled only nine walks and 14 strikeouts. That only two runs were scored on 25 hits shows why. With an extremely high proportion of all hits being singles, dead-ball era pitchers were free to pitch in the strike zone and put the ball in play without risking the catastrophic, game-breaking home run. With little reason to "pitch around" sluggers with curve balls or to throw unhittable "waste pitches" with two strikes, dead-ball era hurlers threw fewer pitches to each batter and worked at a brisk pace.

The most amazing thing about the Boston-Brooklyn game from a modern point of view is that both teams' starting pitchers, Leon Cadore of the Robins and Joe Oeschger of the Braves, stayed in the game for all 26 innings. This was unusual even for those days of iron-man heroics; neither starting catcher was able to go the distance. Coincidentally, Oeschger had survived a 20-inning game the year before and perhaps the experience helped; the veteran righthander allowed a mere nine hits and only once, in the 17th, allowed Brooklyn to put together two hits in an inning. Cadore lived a little more dangerously, allowing 15 hits and relying on superb defensive plays to bail him out of trouble. With one out in the ninth and the bases loaded, second baseman Ivy Olson killed a Boston rally by charging a slow roller, tagging the base runner going by and then getting the force at first. In the sixth, Boston had tied up the score and was threatening to take the lead, but third baseman Boeckel was cut down at the plate by a pair of brilliant throws from the outfield.

For 20 innings the two teams struggled to break the deadlock until umpire McCormick mercifully declared the game suspended on account of darkness. How much longer could Cadore and Oeschger have gone on? Actually, both pitchers were settling into a groove; neither had allowed a run over the final 20 innings or as much as a hit over the final six. Oeschger said in a post-game interview that he had run out of gas in the 18th inning, but that his teammates kept telling him to go "just one more inning, Joe, and we'll get you a run." Cadore claimed that his arm could have lasted a few more innings, but admitted that by the end he was "growing sleepy."

May 1 serves as a microcosm of 1920, a season in which some players and some teams were belting home runs and playing modern, big-bang style baseball, and others were still playing dead ball—hitting for average, bunting, and stealing bases. In 1920 the Yankees hit 115 home runs and stole 64 bases; that same year the Pittsburgh Pirates hit 16 homers and stole 181 bases. Babe Ruth hit 54 home runs while thirteen major-league *teams* hit fewer than 50. It is clear from the numbers that if major-league baseball introduced a rabbit ball in 1920, then most teams were still using the 1919 edition.

THE YEAR: 1922

The number of runs and home runs jumped again in 1922, particularly in the National League, which batted .292 to the AL's .284 and saw its overall ERA rise to a fat 4.10; Shufflin' Phil Douglas of the Giants was the only NL hurler to record an ERA under 3.00. Once again, spitball pitchers Douglas and Red Faber of the White Sox, led both leagues in ERA at 2.63 and 2.80, respectively.

A host of new home-run sluggers challenged the supremacy of the mighty Babe Ruth. In the AL, St. Louis Browns first baseman George Sisler won the batting title at .420—the third-best batting average of the century—and led the league in runs with 134, hits with 246, triples with 18, and even stolen bases with 51. The AL established the modern MVP award, which replaced the defunct Chalmers award, last given in 1914; Sisler won the MVP handily over A's knuckle-ball pitcher Eddie Rommel, who went 27–13 to lead the AL in wins. St. Louis's Ken Williams won the AL home-run title with 39, two more than runner-up Tilly Walker of the Athletics; Williams led in RBIs with 155 and total bases with 367. In the NL, Rogers Hornsby joined the home-run movement by producing the NL's first 20th-century Triple Crown; he hit .401 with 42 home runs and 152 RBIs.

Babe Ruth's season was ruined by an off-the-field battle with new commissioner Landis over a post-World Series barnstorming trip that Landis had ruled illegal. Angry at being openly defied by the Yankees slugger, Landis suspended Ruth and teammate Bob Meusel, who also made the trip, for the first month of the 1922 season. A pouting Ruth batted only .315 with 35 home runs, third-best in the league, in 110 games.

Starting the season without their two best hitters was a huge blow; the Yankees were outscored 867-758

Slick-fielding George Sisler of the St. Louis Browns
won the 1922 MVP award in the AL, leading
the league in batting average, hits, triples,
runs, and stolen bases.

by a Browns team that nipped at their heels all season and even passed them in the standings for a few weeks in midsummer. Besides Sisler and Williams, St. Louis featured William "Baby Doll" Jacobson, who hit .317 with 16 triples, and the AL's best pitching staff, led by 24-game winner Urban Shocker, whose 2.97 ERA was fourth in the league. Nevertheless, in the end the Yankees took the AL flag by one game; a big factor was a new infusion of Red Sox talent, including 26-game winner Joe Bush, pitcher Sad Sam Jones, and shortstop

Everett Scott. Wally Pipp batted .329 with 32 doubles and 10 triples, and Whitey Whitt led the AL in walks with 89 and scored 98 runs.

The 1921 NL pennant winners also repeated in 1922, as the Giants finished seven games ahead of a Cincinnati team led by pitchers Eppa Rixey, who led the NL in wins with 25, and Pete Donohue, who was third in ERA at 3.12. In a rematch of the 1921 Subway Series, this time under a best-of-seven format, Ruth and the Yankees were thrashed again, managing only a game two 3-3 tie out of five games. Giants pitchers Jesse Barnes, Art Nehf, Hugh McQuillan, and Jack Scott, combined ERA 1.76, completely shut down the Yankees lineup; Ruth batted a weak .118 and failed to hit a single home run.

What really explains the changes that occurred in baseball around 1920? A close look at the numbers shows that there is more than one answer to that question. It all started back in the off-season of 1919–20, when the baseball rules committee voted to ban so-called "trick pitches" like the emery ball, scuff ball, shine ball, and, most importantly, the spitball for the upcoming season. All these pitches were considered unsportsmanlike or distasteful because they involved defacing, mutilating, or applying a foreign substance (such as Vaseline, paraffin wax, or actual spit) to the baseball. As with so many other seemingly small changes in the baseball rules, this one changed the game in ways that the men who ran baseball could never have anticipated.

To throw the spitball, the pitcher applies a glob of saliva or other slick substance to the surface of the baseball. He then grips the ball lightly with his first two fingers in contact with the slick spot and throws the pitch with a stiff-wristed delivery, like that used when throwing the knuckle ball. Read by the batter as a fastball, the pitch will dip or break downward at the last minute like a wounded bird; the break of a spitball is as unmistakable as it is effective and bears no resemblance to that of a curve ball or any other conventional breaking pitch. The accepted story of the spitball's invention is that it was first thrown in 1902 by a minor leaguer named Frank Corridon, who passed it on to George Hildebrand (later a major-league umpire), who taught it to Elmer Stricklett. Stricklett brought it to the Chicago White Sox in 1904, where it was picked up by future Hall-of-Famer Ed Walsh, later one of its greatest practitioners. Whether or not this story is true, the pitch does seem to have come onto the baseball scene at around this time.

The spitball pitch was a major reason why pitchers were so dominant in the dead-ball era of the 1900s, and its increased popularity in the middle 1910s may well explain how major-league pitchers were able to adjust so quickly to the introduction of the cork-centered baseball in 1910 and 1911. By the time of the ban in the off-season of 1919–20, the spitter was so entrenched that lifetime exemptions were granted to eight National League and nine American League pitchers who depended on the pitch so much that they would have had to retire otherwise. No one else was allowed to continue using the pitch. The 17 "grandfathered" pitchers, however, continued to throw the spitball throughout the 1920s. Some took extraordinary advantage of their exclusive right to load up the baseball. Spitballers won a remarkable number of ERA titles in both leagues in the 1920s, and quite a few of the original club of 17 achieved unusual longevity in the majors. Jack Quinn pitched until 1933 when he was 49; in 1934 the 42-year-old Burleigh Grimes became the last of the legal spitballers to retire. Counting the modern spitball master Gaylord Perry, at least six primarily spitball pitchers—Grimes, Red Faber, Stan

Coveleski, Ed Walsh, Jack Chesbro, and Perry—have made it to the Baseball Hall of Fame in Cooperstown.

The numbers show that the limited ban of the spitball and the total ban on the other trick pitches that went into effect in 1920 profoundly altered the balance of power between pitchers and hitters. Because most of the legal spitballers were established starting pitchers with workloads of 200 innings per season or more, they provide a perfect control group to study the effect of the spitball ban on the rest of the pitchers in the major leagues. In 1919, the combined ERA of all starting pitchers who were not later included in the group of 17 legal spitballers was 2.75; in 1920 this increased dramatically to 3.30. Interestingly enough, however, the combined ERA of the 17 legal spitballers remained about the same: 2.81 in 1919 and 2.83 in 1920. It was only in 1921 that the ERA of both groups rose; the legal spitballers to 3.48 and the others to 3.73. What would explain these statistics? Certainly not the introduction of a rabbit ball, as a livelier ball would affect spitballers and non-spitballers alike. The most likely explanation is that run-scoring in the major leagues went up so dramatically in 1920 entirely as a result of the preseason rules changes that took several effective pitches away from pitchers' repertoires. If that is difficult to believe, try to imagine the explosion of hitting that would occur in today's game if most pitchers were suddenly prevented from throwing the split-fingered fastball or the slider.

The 1921 numbers indicate that something else happened in that year that further tipped the balance of baseball power toward the hitters, something that affected spitballers and non-spitballers equally. Sure enough, there was a change in 1921 that fits this scenario. As a reaction to the Ray Chapman tragedy of late 1920, for the 1921 season the two major leagues issued new instructions to umpires to throw out discolored, soft baseballs and put in many more fresh new balls. We know from league records that the number of baseballs used per game skyrocketed; this was true for both leagues. Naturally, these newer baseballs were livelier and traveled faster and farther off the bat, whether the pitcher was throwing spitballs, fastballs, curve balls, or any other pitch. It was these two changes, not a new baseball, that, combined with the phenomenon of young power-hitters imitating Babe Ruth's swing-from-the-heels hitting style, are the real culprits in the death of dead-ball baseball.

THE YEAR: 1923

In 1923 John McGraw's NL Giants evicted the Yankees from their newly-renovated home park, the Polo Grounds, where the AL club was outdrawing its landlord by a wide margin. The Yankees responded by building Yankee Stadium, a monumental state-of-the-art facility a Babe Ruth shot or two across the Harlem River in the Bronx. As luck would have it, both teams won their leagues' pennants for the third year in a row.

The Yankees' regular season was a cakewalk. The Bronx Bombers took the AL flag by 16 games over a hard-hitting Detroit Tigers club that featured Harry Heilmann, the batting champ at .403; Ty Cobb, who hit .340 and scored 103 runs; and first baseman Lu Blue, who drew 96 walks to score 100 runs on a .284 batting average. Coming in third by a whisker was Cleveland, the league's top run-scorers with 888 runs, who were paced by 35-year old Tris Speaker's 130 RBIs (tied for league-best with Ruth), 133 runs, and .380 batting average. Cleveland spitballer Stan Coveleski took the ERA title at 2.76, and teammate George Uhle led in wins with 26 and innings pitched with 358. Ruth put together a comeback of sorts, leading the AL in runs with 151, home runs with 41, slugging at .764, and on-

After being evicted by the Giants from the Polo Grounds in 1923, the Yankees began building their own stadium in the Bronx. Yankee Stadium would become known as "the house that Ruth built."

base average at .545; he drew 170 walks, the most by any batter in major-league history, and beat out Eddie Collins for the AL MVP award. In spite of their lumber company image, however, the real backbone of the 1923 Yankee team was pitching. Another Red Sox product, Herb Pennock, went 19–6 for New York to lead the AL in winning percentage, Waite Hoyt was second in

ERA at 3.02, and Sad Sam Jones won 21. The Yankees' 3.66 team ERA led all AL staffs.

The other New York team did lead its league in runs scored, with 854, but the Giants' attack accomplished this without a dominant slugger like Ruth. Ross Youngs batted .336 with a league-high 121 runs scored; Frankie Frisch was fifth in hitting at .348, scored 116 runs and drove in 111; and Emil "Irish" Meusel (Bob's brother) led the NL in RBIs with 125. Once again, New York beat out a tough Cincinnati Reds team that compiled an ERA of 3.21 thanks to a career year from Dolf Luque, one of the first Cubans to star in the major leagues. Luque led the NL in wins with 27, shutouts with six, winning percentage at .771, and ERA at a dead-ballesque 1.93. In a year when two whole NL teams batted in the .290s, the league hit only .235 off Luque. St. Louis Cardinals second baseman Rogers Hornsby won the batting title at .384, beating out teammate Jim Bottomley by 13 points, but his heroics had little impact on the pennant race; the Cardinals finished at 79–74, 16 games out. Cy Williams's league-leading 41 home runs mattered even less, as his Phillies lost 104 games to come in last.

Colorful Giants outfielder Casey Stengel hit Yankee Stadium's first-ever World Series homer, an inside-the-park job with two out in the bottom of the ninth that gave Rosy Ryan a 5-4 victory over the Yankees' Joe Bush; he also homered in game three. But the Yankees finally broke the Giants' spell to win games four, five, and six and win the series, four games to two. Ruth batted .368 with three home runs, and his team batted .293.

The home-run revolution continued to transform major-league baseball throughout the 1920s. The power of Babe Ruth and his imitators gradually put pitchers on the defensive and swept away all of the nuances and subtle beauty of "scientific baseball." Run totals soared. Pitchers pitched scared; the average number of pitches per at-bat rose, and arms burned out. By the end of the decade, major-league managers were asking their starters to throw 250 or 260 innings in a season, not the 325 or 350 innings of the early part of the decade. The sacrifice bunt and the hit-and-run play fell out of favor. After all, why give the opposing team an out or ask a hitter to cut down on his swing when one long flyball could win a ball game? The same went for base stealing; stolen-base totals plummeted in the 1920s, as managers gradually realized that base runners could score just as easily from first base as from second on a homer. Home runs, of course, were becoming easier and easier to come by; the AL hit 160 homers in 1915 and 439 in 1927. So were all kinds of hits; in 1915 nine major-league hitters batted .300 or better; in 1927 35 reached the .300 mark. Of the ten 20th-century seasons in which a major-league batter has batted .400 or better, an incredible six of them came between 1920 and 1929.

There is absolutely no question that Babe Ruth and home-run baseball were a tremendous success. It may well have saved the major leagues, considering how disillusioned many fans had become after the Black Sox scandal. In any case, after a half-decade of no growth, major-league attendance exploded. After drawing a little over five million fans in 1917, the 16 major-league teams drew more than eight million three times during the 1920s and more than nine million seven times. Babe Ruth himself became famous throughout the country and the entire world. The appeal of Ruth and the other home-run hitters was eloquently described by Heywood Broun when he wrote: "Whenever a player hits a ball out of the park I have a sense of elation. I feel as if I had done it. To me, every wall or fence is palpably an inhibition. Beyond the bleacher roof lies Italy."[2]

To hold the immense crowds of fans that paid to share this feeling, the New York Yankees built the first grand baseball stadium, as distinct from a mere baseball park.

The marriage of baseball and the electronic media dates to this era. The World Series of 1920 was witnessed by only a few thousand fans and a couple of hundred thousand more via telegraph reports transmitted to men's clubs and barrooms. In 1922, however, five million people listened to the series live on the radio. By the end of the decade, the first great radio networks were bringing live or recreated baseball games to many millions of people in every corner of the United States. Major-league baseball stars became objects of greater hero-worship than ever. The national pastime had never been more national, not to mention more popular or profitable.

Like most great changes, those that baseball went through in the 1920s were not universally welcomed. Just as their counterparts at the turn of the century complained about the disappearance of slugging and run-scoring, some baseball men of the 1920s mourned the loss of the dead-ball era traditions of complex offensive teamwork and dominating pitching. Sounding almost like an Englishman complaining that hitting the long ball "isn't cricket," *Baseball Magazine* correspondent F.C. Lane cast Babe Ruth as a villain who was ruining baseball by encouraging mindless slugging over finesse and skill. "Almost any batter," Lane wrote glumly in 1921, "that has it in him to wallop the ball is swinging from the handle of the bat with every ounce of strength that nature placed in his wrist and shoulders." The most influential of these purists was sportswriter-turned-fiction-writer Ring Lardner, who soured on major-league baseball during the 1920s and eventually quit writing about the game.

Originally a beat writer covering the Cubs and White Sox for the *Chicago Tribune,* Ring Lardner was the leading light of a generation of great writers who covered baseball with unequaled style during the dead-ball era. It was an era in which few fans had the time or money to visit major-league parks in person and in which there was no film, TV, or radio coverage of baseball games. What the dead-ball era could offer fans outside the ballpark was daily newspaper coverage written by a group of the greatest literary craftsmen who have ever worn a press badge. Besides Lardner there was Hughie Fullerton, Franklin P. Adams, Fred Lieb, Grantland Rice, Heywood Broun, and Damon Runyon. In addition to their journalism, these men left behind a legacy of great baseball biographies and histories; many of them outgrew sports writing to produce short stories, plays, and novels that are still read and admired today.

A confirmed misanthrope, or person who despises humankind, Lardner saw in baseball a world where— unlike most other areas of life—incompetence, phoni-ness, and evil were exposed to everyone's view and where virtue, hard work, and talent stood at least a chance of coming out on top. He was also a bit of an elitist, and he loved "inside baseball," the idea that only those with a discerning eye and enough experience to appreciate the game in all its fine details and percent-ages could truly understand it. Two things helped to destroy Lardner's love of baseball. One was the Black Sox scandal, which revealed depths of evil and corrup-tion in the national game that shocked and disillu-sioned even a cynic like Lardner. The other was the advent of Babe Ruth and big-bang baseball, which was about as subtle as a fireworks display. Ring Lardner's idea of a great baseball club was the 1914 Miracle Braves, who came from behind to win the NL pennant and a world championship without having one really first-rate star. "I say the Braves won by hustlin' and fightin' rather than because they was an aggregation of world beaters," he once wrote, "the kind o' men that can do their best in a pinch is the kind that's most valuable in baseball or anywhere else. They're worth more than the guys that's got all the ability in the world but can't find it when they want it."

What Lardner hated about Ruth was that he had "all the ability in the world" and that he could find it when he wanted it. Babe Ruth may have saved baseball from the boredom and corruption of the dead-ball era and restored the faith of as many fans as Kenesaw Mountain Landis, but to Lardner it was Ruth and his kind of baseball that was corrupt. Lardner was a believer in the "rabbit ball" theory, and he was convinced that the baseball "magnates" had changed the baseball on purpose and "fixed up [the game] to please the public with their usual good judgment." As Lardner wrote in a 1930 article explaining why he abandoned baseball as played with the "Br'er Rabbit ball":

> I have always been a fellow who liked to see efficiency rewarded. If a pitcher pitched a swell game, I wanted to see him win it. So it kind of sickens me to watch a typical pastime of today in which a good pitcher, after an hour and fifty minutes of deserved mastery of his opponents, can suddenly be made to look like a bum by four or five great sluggers who couldn't have held a job as bat boy on the Niles High School scrubs.[3]

CHAPTER FIVE

Oh, You Kid: Babe Ruth's America

The story of George Herman "Babe" Ruth is an American original. Almost every aspect of it is improbable or one-of-a-kind. Like other great heroes Ruth attracted all kinds of tall tales, myths, and legends. Unlike most of them, however, it is hard to say which is more outrageous or entertaining—the true stories about the Babe or the false ones. Even the truth about Ruth could sound far-fetched. In the 1960s, former major-leaguer Tommy Holmes said that he had stopped telling stories about things he had seen Ruth do 30 years earlier "for the simple reason that I realized that those who had never seen him didn't believe me."

The only typical thing about the story of Babe Ruth is his family background. Like most ballplayers of the early 20th century, Ruth came from the lower end of the working class. At the time of his birth in 1895 his father, George, Sr., ran a saloon in Baltimore's tough waterfront district—very close to the present site of Camden Yards, the AL Baltimore Orioles' new ballpark. Since both of his parents worked long hours, the young

Ruth was left more or less unsupervised to pass his days wandering the docks, stealing from passing wagons, and learning how to swear, smoke, and chew. Ruth later claimed that he drank beer and chewed tobacco expertly before he knew how to read. What made things worse for Ruth and his family was that by his nature, young George needed more supervision than most children; he was born with a tendency toward wildness and excess. Other kids got into minor scrapes or committed minor acts of mischief; George repeatedly got into the biggest trouble available and built up an impressive criminal record before he got out of grammar school. Regular horsewhippings by George, Sr., seemed to have little effect. By the time Ruth was seven, his family gave up, had him declared "incorrigible," and turned him over to St. Mary's Industrial School for Boys, a combination boarding school and reformatory run by the Xaverian Brothers, a fraternal Catholic order.

When his father dropped him off at St. Mary's imposing front gate on a June day in 1902, Ruth cried pitifully and begged to be taken home, but George, Sr., did not flinch. Even though Babe Ruth would see little of his family over the next 12 years, the Xaverian Brothers were the best thing that could have happened to him. Without the education, attention, and rigorous discipline that he received at St. Mary's it is likely that Ruth would have spent most of the rest of his life in prison, not reveling in the adulation of millions of baseball fans and earning more money than Cap Anson, King Kelly, and Ty Cobb put together.

The philosophy of St. Mary's was that every boy could succeed at something; the school offered a wide variety of academic and vocational courses of study. After a few years at the school, Ruth discovered a gift for tailoring. With the skills he developed there—reportedly, he could produce a finished shirt from whole cloth in a mere 15 minutes—he could have earned a very comfortable living as a master shirt maker. Soon, however, George Ruth found another application for his amazing eyesight and eye-to-hand coordination: baseball. The Xaverian Brothers loved baseball and ran an extensive intramural baseball program; St. Mary's best nine were regular contenders for the Baltimore city championship. One brother in particular, Brother Matthias, recognized Ruth's natural ability and took him under his wing. Like Ruth, Brother Matthias was exceptionally big, tall, and strong. By the time he was 16, Ruth was a sensation as a left-handed catcher and part-time pitcher. Especially noticeable about Ruth was the powerful uppercut swing that he copied from Brother Matthias, who was locally renowned for his tremendous one-handed fungoes, or fly balls hit for outfield practice. The first seed of baseball's great home run revolution of the 1920s may have been Ruth's childish attempt to imitate every mannerism of his favorite coach and teacher.

When Ruth was 15 he was discharged to a hostel run by the school in Baltimore, and a job was found for him as a shirtmaker. Within two months, however, he had returned to St. Mary's a failure—not at his trade but at leading an independent life; Ruth had fallen in with a bad crowd and was wasting his earnings on drinking, smoking, and night life. According to the reminiscences of Ruth's teachers, the teenaged Ruth's problems were more the result of high spirits and immaturity than malice. They remembered that he never tried to escape punishment by telling a lie, that he was protective toward younger children, and that he liked to fritter away his savings on boxes of candy that he would pass out to friends. Back at St. Mary's, the plan was for him to earn another chance at freedom and eventually resume his career. By the time he was 18, however, Babe Ruth's life had taken a different direction. He was already sure that baseball, not making shirts, was to be his destiny in life.

In 1913 Ruth attracted the attention of professional baseball. He batted .537 for the season and decisively defeated college star and future major-leaguer Bill Morrisette in a late-season exhibition game attended by pro scouts, including Jack Dunn, the owner of the Baltimore Orioles. The Orioles were a top minor-league club that produced a steady stream of first-rate baseball talent, including such big-league superstars as Lefty Grove, Ernie Shore, Max Bishop, and George Earnshaw. Babe Ruth was better than any of them. It is a telling commentary on the pitching and defense mind-set of dead-ball era baseball men that Dunn refused to consider signing Ruth as anything but a pitcher. Dunn's first words upon seeing Ruth were: "There is a Rube Waddell in the rough." Brother Matthias protested that Ruth was an even better hitter—Ruth was already legendary for how far he could hit St. Mary's battered old baseballs—but all Dunn wanted to know was: "But can he pitch?" Ruth signed a professional contract with the Orioles and left St. Mary's for good on February 27, 1914. Since he was still a minor, Jack Dunn took over Ruth's legal guardianship from the school. During spring training, Ruth was referred to as "Jack Dunn's babe" and by Opening Day the nickname had stuck. From then on he was Babe Ruth.

During that first spring training Ruth hit his first professional home run in Fayetteville, North Carolina, and created a local sensation with his awesome extra-base hits. Unmoved, Dunn told a reporter that Ruth was "not only a slugger, but a great pitcher." It is true that Ruth shined in seven mound appearances against major-league clubs, beating the Phillies, Dodgers, and A's. His success continued into the regular season of 1914, but that was the first year of the war waged against the major-league monopoly by the Federal League, which

*Jack Dunn (left), pictured here with Commissioner
Landis and John McGraw, signed up 19-year-old
Babe Ruth as a pitcher for his minor-league club,
the Baltimore Orioles.*

planted a major-league franchise—the Terrapins—literally across the street from Dunn's park. Attendance at Orioles games plummeted, and Dunn was forced to sell most of his stars to stay afloat. This is how it happened that Babe Ruth landed in the American League Boston Red Sox' pitching rotation in 1915.

Off the field, Babe Ruth was still behaving the way he always had when no one was watching over him, only now he had more money. He ate, smoked, and drank too much. He used one of his first Boston paychecks to buy a car, got into an accident, and had his driver's license revoked. As part of his daily routine, Ruth ate breakfast at Landers coffee shop in Boston; one day he turned to his regular waitress, a pretty, dark-haired girl named Helen Woodford, and said: "How about you and me getting married?" She accepted and became the first Mrs. George Herman Ruth. The Babe was 19; Helen was 16. The marriage was short-lived and did little to settle Ruth down while it lasted. Helen died in a fire in 1929, but by that time she and Ruth had been estranged for many years, and Ruth immediately married his girlfriend Claire Hodgson. In spring training in Hot Springs, Arkansas—then a wide-open gambling mecca—he discovered the pleasures of faro, horses, and roulette and lost, in the words of a teammate, "more [money] than he had coming for the whole season." Throughout the 1915 season, Ruth was regularly fined and suspended by Red Sox manager Bill "Rough" Carrigan for breaking the team's midnight curfew. As the story goes, the first time Ruth was caught returning to the hotel in the early morning, he told Carrigan with a straight face that he had been in his room at midnight like he was supposed to be, but that he went out again at quarter past. Driving without a license late one night in 1917, Ruth tried to thread the needle between a pair of converging trolley cars but did not make it. The car was totaled and an unidentified woman in the passenger seat, not Helen Ruth, was seriously hurt. Ruth survived without a scratch.

On the mound, however, Ruth was mature beyond his years, and none of his excesses had yet caught up with him. Fast, fit, and strong as an ox, the Babe Ruth of 1915–19 bore no resemblance to the pudgy, barrel-chested figure known to today's fans from photographs taken in the late 1920s and 1930s. By the late 1910s Ruth was one of the best pitchers on the best team in the American League. In 1915 Ruth went 18–8 with an ERA of 2.44, but manager Carrigan got even with Ruth for all the curfew violations and other headaches by

Babe Ruth limbers up his pitching arm before a Red Sox game. Although he became famous as a slugger, Ruth compiled an impressive record as a pitcher and even won the AL's ERA title in 1916.

benching him in the World Series in favor of veterans Rube Foster, Ernie Shore, Dutch Leonard, and Smokey Joe Wood. Ruth was furious. The 1916 season was Ruth's finest hour, as he went 23–12 and beat out Walter Johnson, Jim Bagby, Harry Coveleski, Eddie Cicotte, Bob Shawkey, and his Red Sox teammates to win the ERA title at 1.75. Over the next two years, Ruth went 24–13 and 13–7, respectively, but by 1918 Ruth was finally beginning to attract more attention for his hitting than his pitching. (Of course, pitchers hit for themselves in those days; the DH rule would not be adopted by the AL until 1973.) In 1917 he achieved the rare distinction, even rarer for a pitcher, of completing an entire season without being pinch-hit for once. That year Ruth also made headlines for punching umpire Brick Owen in the jaw after Owen called Ruth's first four pitches of a game balls. This game has gone down in the baseball record book, although not for anything Ruth did; after Ruth was ejected, Ernie Shore came in, picked off Ruth's base runner, and then threw nine perfect innings.

Making spot appearances at first base, in the out-field, and as a pinch-hitter for other Boston pitchers, in 1918 Ruth swatted 11 triples and 11 homers to win his first home-run title. Fans all over the AL thrilled at Ruth's aggressiveness at the plate, and he was cheered even when striking out. Called "the caveman of base-ball" by the *New York Times,* Ruth swung his bat "like the men of the stone age waved their mighty clubs." As these words were written, Ed Barrow had taken over as manager of the Red Sox. Barrow is the man who would eventually move Ruth into the everyday line-up for good; in early 1918, however, he was not ready even to consider the possibility. "I'd be the laughingstock of baseball," he said, like a true dead-ball era baseball man, "if I changed the best left hander in the game into an outfielder."

By 1919 Babe Ruth was well on his way to a Hall-of-Fame career as a starting pitcher. He was only 25. Barring a serious injury, it is easy to imagine him with a lifetime ERA under 3.00 and 300 or more career victories. After all, he had won 65 games in only three seasons as a full-time major-league pitcher. Ruth's career, however, was about to take another 90-degree turn. As good a pitcher as he was, in 1919 Ruth returned to his first love, hitting, and as popular as he was in Boston, in 1920 he would leave the Red Sox for the New York Yankees. Interestingly enough, both of these moves were made for reasons that had little directly to do with baseball. In 1918 the United States entered World War I and the government ordered all able-bodied young men to "work or fight," meaning to get a job in a war-related industry or risk being drafted into the Armed Forces. In 1918 and 1919 baseball players left the game in droves; the Red Sox were hit particularly hard, losing Jack Barry, Duffy Lewis, and several other players. The Red Sox borrowed Stuffy McInnis and three other members of the Philadelphia Athletics, and manager Barrow was forced to play his ace left-hander, who was exempt from the draft as a married man, in the outfield.

In his 432 at-bats Babe Ruth surprised everyone in the country, with the possible exception of Brother Matthias, by launching 29 home runs to break Socks Seybold's AL record by 13 and the major-league record by two. The old major-league record was 27, set in 1884 by Ned Williamson of Cap Anson's old Chicago Colts. But Williamson's record was a phony, more a product of an irrational grounds rule than athletic achievement. The Colts played for two seasons in a tiny park where the distance to the right field wall was a mere 215 feet from home plate or about 150 feet closer than the "Green Monster," the inviting left-field wall in today's cozy Fenway Park. In the first year in which the

Colts played there, a fly ball into the right-field stands counted as a double; in 1884 the team experimented with counting the same fly ball as a home run. Ruth hit his 29 homers playing in old Fenway Park which, unlike the modern version, was one of the toughest hitter's parks in the majors; the Red Sox hit only 10 home runs at home all year; opposing batters hit a league-low three.

The primary reason for Babe Ruth's 1920 sale to the Yankees was Boston owner and theatrical promoter Harry Frazee's money troubles. In 1919 Frazee's show business ventures were deep in debt, and the once-profitable Red Sox were proving a financial disappointment. Attendance was down because of the war, and the shortened 1918 season and the 1918 World Series had not made a dime; Frazee was having trouble making the payments he still owed the previous Boston owner, Joseph Lannin. Desperate, he turned to Jacob Ruppert and Tillinghast Huston, the wealthy owners of the Yankees, who agreed to buy Ruth for $100,000 in cash and notes—double the highest amount ever paid for a major-league player—and a $300,000 loan backed by a mortgage on the Red Sox' Fenway Park. As things turned out, the complex Babe Ruth deal worked out well for both sides. The Yankees got Ruth and several other Red Sox stars over the years in lieu of payments on the Fenway mortgage; and Frazee stayed financially afloat long enough to score big with his 1925 Broadway mega-hit *No, No, Nanette*. The only losers were the fans of Boston and the Red Sox themselves. The team won five world championships between 1903 and 1918; it has yet to win a single World Series in the 78 years since.

The Red Sox never knew what they had in Babe Ruth. During Ruth's five seasons in Boston the club kept him out of a World Series, bickered with him about his private life, nickel-and-dimed him in salary talks, and insisted on using him as a pitcher against Ruth's wishes. Even after the 1919 season, Boston management talked of returning Babe Ruth to the pitching rotation. Most absurd of all was Frazee's idea of selling Ruth because of declining fan attendance; as Ruth was shortly to prove, he could sell many times more tickets than Ruppert and Huston had dollars. The Yankees, on the other hand, paid Ruth astronomical sums of money, put him in the outfield, batted him third, and left him alone. There he became, in the words of contemporary sportswriter Fred Lieb: "with the exception of King David of Israel, whose slingshot knockout of Goliath is recorded in millions of bibles printed in hundreds of languages, . . . the most publicized athlete who ever lived."[1]

Critics of the home-run revolution and opposing AL pitchers were just about the only Americans who did not get a huge kick out of Babe Ruth's monster hitting performances of 1920 and 1921. Ruth hit 54 home runs in his first year as a Yankee and drove in a league-leading 137 runs; his .847 slugging average remains the best seasonal slugging mark in baseball history. He further dismayed dead-ball apologists like Ring Lardner by out-hitting the great Ty Cobb for average, .376 to .334, walking 148 times, and scoring an AL-high 158 runs; he even stole 14 bases. Ruth produced a carbon copy of this season the following year, as he batted .378, slugged .846, and swatted an unthinkable 59 balls over AL fences. On June 10, 1921, at the age of 26, Babe Ruth tied the career home-run record of 119 set by Phillies' slugger Gavvy "Cactus" Cravath, who led the NL in homers six times between 1908 and 1920. Babe Ruth had single-handedly propelled the New York Yankees to their first pennant and brought hundreds of thousands of new fans into baseball; Yankee home attendance more than doubled and overall AL attendance rose by almost one million fans. In 1921, accord-

This stop-action sequence shows the Babe's trademark uppercut swing.

ing to historian Lee Allen, "[Babe Ruth] was as much a tourist attraction in New York City as the Statue of Liberty, Grant's Tomb, and the Fulton Fish Market." A candy company cashed in on Ruth-mania with a hot-selling new candy bar called the "Baby Ruth," claiming, weakly, that the bar was named after former president Grover Cleveland's daughter. The Yankees made extra millions by playing exhibition games around the country featuring, of course, "guaranteed" appearances by Babe Ruth. Newspapers everywhere carried a syndicated feature called "What Babe Ruth Did Today." The Yankees had given him a 100 percent raise over his Red Sox salary of $10,000 when they acquired him in 1920; in 1922 they gave him a five-year contract worth $52,000 per year.

Like everyone else, Ruth's teammates on the Yankees were in awe of his baseball skills, but only they knew how little Ruth slept and how much he ate, drank, and smoked with no apparent effect on his on-field performance. "What a fantastic ballplayer he was," remembered teammate Joe Dugan, "the things he could do. But he wasn't human. He dropped out of a tree." As if in reaction to the poverty of his childhood and the extreme discipline at St. Mary's, Babe Ruth spent money, chased women, and consumed luxuries as if every day was his last on earth. He smoked fine Havana cigars until he was blue in the face. There are stories about him putting away 18 eggs and six slices of toast for breakfast. Ty Cobb once said:

> I've seen him at midnight, propped up in bed, order six club sandwiches, a platter of pig's knuckles, and a pitcher of beer. He'd down all that while smoking a big black cigar. Next day, if he hit a homer, he'd trot around the bases complaining about gas pains and a belly-ache . . . How that man could eat![2]

Outfielder Ping Bodie, who had been the Yankees' unofficial eating champion, conceded his title to Ruth, saying, "Anybody who eats three pounds of steak and a bottle of chili sauce for a starter has got me." On road trips to St. Louis, one of his favorite eating spots, Ruth would buy piles of barbecued ribs and cases of beer; he would then take over a washroom on the Yankees' train and sell them to his fellow passengers at fifty cents a portion, beer included. He treated sports cars and silk shirts as if they were disposable tissues. As for his love of night life, Bodie, who was Ruth's roommate in 1921, got off this famous line: "I don't room with him. I room with his suitcase." His tremendous appetite extended to women as well, although unlike many modern so-called sports heroes, Ruth was never accused of abusing or taking advantage of a woman in any way. As his second wife Claire put it, "The presence of the Babe in any town gave a lot of odd females telephonitis . . . [He] brought out the beast in a lot of ladies the world over."

The Yankees owners took an indulgent attitude toward Babe Ruth's excesses. After all, according to Yankees shortstop Roger Peckinpaugh, "he liked the night life, but was always at the park early the next day in time for batting practice and in good shape to play." Not so little Miller Huggins, the 5'6", 140-pound former second baseman whom Jacob Ruppert hired as Yankees manager in 1918. Huggins tried to bully Ruth into cutting down on his off-field activities, but Ruth would not have it. Derisively addressing Huggins to his face as "little boy," Ruth ignored Huggins's orders and lost few opportunities to remind his manager what would happen if he went to Ruppert and Huston and insisted that one of them had to go. There is a famous story that Ruth once held Huggins upside by the heels and dangled him, terrified, off the back of a moving railroad train.

Babe Ruth may have been a glutton, an unfaithful husband, and a hard drinker, but he had a good side. Like many of the Brothers of St. Mary's, Ruth's teammates may not have approved of how he behaved, but they genuinely liked him. Ruth had a big heart and sincerely loved children. He frequently returned to St. Mary's bearing gifts and donations for the school and the Xaverian Brothers, including several automobiles, and enjoyed visiting other orphanages and children's hospitals. The famous sentimental story of the Babe visiting a sick boy in the hospital, promising to hit him a home run in that day's game, and then delivering is actually true. It is a testament to Ruth's basic charm and goodheartedness that his friendships with men from much different backgrounds, men such as the urbane Waite Hoyt or the mild-mannered Herb Pennock, survived Ruth's childlike undependability and his unfamiliarity with the social graces. Pennock told the story of a formal dinner attended by Ruth and a group of other teammates and their wives during which Ruth got up and announced: "Excuse me, I've got to take a piss." Pennock then followed him to the men's room and explained that it was impolite to talk like that in mixed company. When Ruth returned to the table, he turned to the women and said, sweetly, "I'm sorry I said 'piss.'"

Two of Ruth's most infuriating and most endearing qualities were his utter lack of pretense and his inability to remember people's names. Babe Ruth simply did not much care who or what anybody else was. It certainly was not that he had a poor memory; Ruth was known for his ability to recall pitchers' tendencies or the exact circumstances of a home run that he had hit ten years earlier. According to Waite Hoyt, when Hoyt left the Yankees in 1930 after 11 seasons as Ruth's teammate, best friend, and drinking buddy, a solemn Ruth shook his hand and said, "Good bye, Walter." This obliviousness extended to the rich and famous as well. When

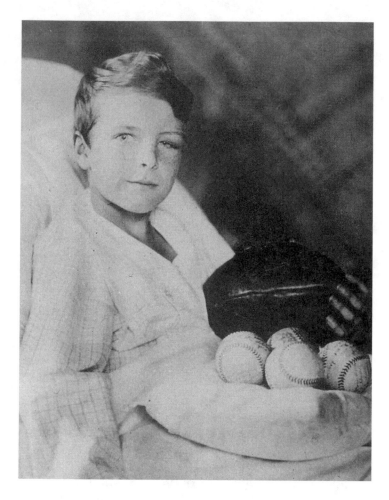

*Johnny Sylvester shows off the gifts brought to him
by Babe Ruth, who promised to hit a home run
for the ailing youngster that day—and did.*

Herb Pennock once asked Ruth who he had had dinner
with the night before, Ruth replied, "Oh, some movie
people." When asked what movie people, he said,
"Oh, you know, what the hell are their names?" Ruth
had spent the evening with Mary Pickford and Douglas

Fairbanks—two movie superstars who at that time were bigger than Humphrey Bogart, Jack Nicholson, and Robert Redford put together. When introduced to a uniformed and bemedaled Marshal Ferdinand Foch, the French commander of the allied forces, at a celebration of the allied victory in World War I, Ruth broke the ice by saying, "Hey Gen, they tell me you were in the war."

If Babe Ruth thought that there was no one in baseball who could make him toe the line, he found out after the 1921 season that he was very wrong. There was one: Kenesaw Mountain Landis. One of Landis's first objectives as commissioner was to raise the status of the annual World Series from a mere post-season exhibition to something much more glamorous and prestigious, a fitting showcase for America's national pastime. To that end he made it clear that he would enforce the old rule forbidding World Series participants from playing any other off-season exhibition or barnstorming games on the grounds that they might detract from the drama of the series. Ruth and several teammates ignored Landis's warning and signed contracts to go on a barnstorming tour following the final game of the 1921 series. When the news reached Landis he made an angry phone call to Ruth and ordered him to back out of the tour. When Ruth insisted that he would go, Landis told him, "If you do, it will be the sorriest thing you've ever done in baseball."

Despite the pleas of Yankee owners Ruppert and Huston, Babe Ruth went through with the exhibition tour, saying: "Aw, let the old guy jump in a lake." In December, Landis withheld Ruth's World Series check and suspended him without pay for the first 39 days of the 1922 season. All kinds of pressure was put on Landis to lighten the punishment, but he held fast. "[Ruth] gets away with a lot in the American League," Landis said, "but in this office, he's just another player." The Yankees won their second straight AL pennant in 1922, but with Ruth missing a month-and-a-half of action and then sulking his way to a .315 batting average and only 35 home runs, they barely slipped past the St. Louis Browns by one game in the standings. Ruth set the tone for the Yankees in the postseason as well; he batted under .200 with no homers and the Yankees were swept by John McGraw's New York Giants in four straight games.

Babe Ruth bounced back stronger than ever in 1923, hitting 41 homers and batting a Cobbian .393, the best batting average of his 22-year career. He then went on to avenge the World Series losses of 1921 and 1922 by battering the New York Giants' pitching staff; Ruth hit .368 and smashed three home runs as the Yankees won their first world championship, four games to two. In 1923 Ruth also received another great tribute when sportswriter Fred Lieb nicknamed the Yankees' new Bronx ballpark "The House That Ruth Built."

Tired of seeing their tenants outdraw them in their own park and deprive them of a loyal home crowd in the World Series of 1921 and 1922, the New York Giants finally evicted Ruth's Yankees after the 1922 season. "If we kick them out," John McGraw gloated, "they won't be able to find another location on Manhattan Island. . . . The fans will forget about them and they'll be through." McGraw was right on one count—there were no longer any ballpark-sized undeveloped lots for sale in Manhattan—but dead wrong on the second. Yankees owners Ruppert and Huston bought ten acres directly across the Harlem River from the Polo Grounds and on May 5, 1922, broke ground on the grandest, most extravagant baseball park ever conceived. Because the terms "ballpark," "field," and "grounds" seemed somehow inadequate to the grandeur of their design, the Yankees decided to call their new home Yankee Stadium, the first time that term was used for a baseball facility. Finished in a mere 284 days, the stadium featured an awesome 58,000 seats divided among three vast decks. With its stately outer facade, interior copper frieze, and a majestic, sweeping grandstand that curved around its immense outfield, Yankee Stadium reminded many of its first visitors of the Colosseum in Rome. On Opening Day of 1923, 74,000 fans filled the stadium to break the major-league attendance record (47,373, set at Boston's Braves Field in game two of the 1916 World Series) by a Ruthian margin. An estimated 25,000 others were turned away.

In the fourth inning of that first game, Babe Ruth surprised no one by christening the new ballpark with a tie-breaking three-run home run into the right-field bleachers. It was during his report of this game that Fred Lieb coined the stadium's immortal nickname, which seemed only more fitting as time went on. Seeming to feed off the energy of great crowds, Ruth continued to hit clutch homer after clutch homer in the new park. A look at the Yankees' financial books from those days would probably show that if Ruth did not literally build Yankee Stadium, he certainly paid for the new park in increased ticket sales. And he was good business not only for the Yankees, but for the whole AL and the rest of professional baseball as well; his personal heroics and the home-run revolution that he spearheaded caused an explosion in the popularity and profitability of baseball all across the country. Hard-core baseball fans may have loved dead ball, but the phenomenon of Babe Ruth turned nearly every American of the 1920s into a baseball fan. Ruth's fellow players benefited, too; between 1920 and 1923, the average major-league salary rose more than 30 percent. As Yankees pitcher Waite Hoyt often said, "Every big leaguer should teach his children to pray: 'God bless Mommy. God bless Daddy. And God bless Babe Ruth.'"

Ruth and the Yankees kept right on rolling through the middle 1920s. In 1924, 1926, and 1927—when Ruth was 32, middle-aged for a baseball player—the

The Babe is mobbed by a crowd of fans.

Babe put up three of the kind of seasons that the public had come to expect from him. He batted .378, .372, and .356 with 46, 47, and 60 homers, respectively. During those years the New York Yankees won two AL pennants and another world championship. In 1925, however, Babe Ruth suffered a rude awakening bigger than the 39-game suspension and lost season of 1922. This time it did not take the form of a stubborn white-haired judge from Chicago; in 1925 Babe Ruth was sent a loud message of protest from his own taken-for-granted and much-abused body.

It started during the Yankees' annual spring training trip to Hot Springs, Arkansas. Every year, Ruth had showed up a little bit fatter, but in 1925 his weight had ballooned to an unhealthy 230 pounds. Jogging and bicycling extra hard to try to get in shape, Ruth experienced a mysterious fainting spell. This was followed by another fainting episode on the train trip north to New York. He looked pale and complained that every bone in his body ached. As soon as the Yankees reached the city, Ruth was rushed to St. Vincent's hospital and a wild rumor that he had died swept the country and the world. As he was being carried into the hospital Ruth suffered a series of violent convulsions and had to be restrained. After he was sedated and admitted, one of his doctors suggested to reporters that Ruth's illness was related to his excessive eating and drinking. "He's very careless," the doctor added.

Even though Babe Ruth spent several weeks in the hospital, the public was never told exactly what was wrong with him; we still do not know for sure today. The press called Ruth's illness "the bellyache heard around the world" and made jokes about Ruth's incredible eating capacity. His doctors talked at various times of "influenza," "indigestion," and "indiscreet eating." He was operated on, supposedly for an "abscess." Rumors persist to this day, however, that Ruth's real problem was, as a teammate put it, "something a bit lower" than the stomach—meaning syphilis or another sexually-transmitted disease. Whatever was really wrong, the press suddenly began to act as if it were open season on the Babe's private life. Reporters pestered Helen Ruth with questions about Claire Hodgson and other women linked romantically to Ruth; Helen soon joined her husband in the hospital and was treated for a "nervous condition." Newspapers ran revealing stories about Ruth's off-field misbehavior, including allegations that he had gambled on baseball, that he had paid large sums of money to extortionists, that he was in trouble with bookmakers, and that he was flat broke.

After a long, slow recovery Ruth returned to action on June 1. At the end of August, however, manager Huggins suspended him and fined him the then-unprecedented amount of $5,000 for, in Huggins's words: "misconduct, drinking, and staying out all night." Ruth howled that "bootleggers" did not receive fines that large, but he soon discovered that the press which had once protected him was undergoing one of its periodic bouts of pomposity. Ruth was charged and found guilty of being a fallen role model and "letting down America's kids."

There is no question that he had let down the New York Yankees. When the 1925 season ended, the formerly invincible pinstripers had compiled an abysmal record of 69–85 to finish 28½ games behind a first-place Washington club led by dead-ball survivor Walter Johnson, who went 20–7 at the age of 37. The Yankees had only Boston's even more disastrous 47–105 performance to thank for keeping them out of the very bottom of the AL cellar. Ruth himself batted a very ordinary .290 with 25 home runs and 66 RBIs. Editorial writers danced on his grave. "What has the future in store for Babe Ruth?" one New York paper wrote. "It is doubtful that Ruth again will be the super-star that he was from 1919 to 1924. By next year he will be 32 and the Babe at 32 will be much older than Eddie Collins, Walter Johnson, and Ty Cobb were at that age."

CHAPTER SIX

*B*iz, Pop, and Smokey Joe: Race, Baseball, and the Founding of the Negro Leagues

Professional baseball has always closely reflected American racial attitudes. The bigoted, class-conscious Northeasterners who founded the first amateur baseball clubs refused to admit African-Americans into their clubs, leagues, or organizations. Racial attitudes in baseball relaxed considerably during the 1880s, a time of substantial thawing in race relations in most regions of the country; it was then that 60 or so African-Americans appeared in the minor leagues and the African-American Walker brothers played briefly in the majors. In the 1890s and early 1900s, a wave of white supremacism, or the philosophy that people of European descent are inherently superior to African-Americans, entered the American political mainstream and swept away the racial progress of previous decades. Great African-American players like Sol White, Rube Foster, Bud Fowler, George Stovey, and Frank Grant—many of whom had played on integrated teams in the minor leagues—were pushed back into the world of African-American baseball.

White supremacist ideas, including enforced segregation, or separation of the races, reached their absolute peak in American history between 1900 and 1930. This was especially true in the South, which missed out on some of the positive trends of the time such as immigration and urban growth. As a result, the South became increasingly isolated both culturally and economically. The Ku Klux Klan, which had died out in the 1860s, revived in 1915 in Georgia and rode virtually unchallenged by the federal government. Anti-African-American violence became more and more common; in the first quarter of the 20th century, the term "race riot" was more likely to mean white-on-black violence than violent African-American protest. Following the election victory of a white supremacist politician in Atlanta in 1906, white mobs rioted for four days, looting, burning, and attacking African-Americans at random. Across the South, Jim Crow laws were passed to keep the races apart by providing separate railroad cars, restaurants, rest rooms, and other public accommodations. As time went on, these were refined and extended to cover the most trivial activities. Many local governments required separate public elevators for whites and African-Americans and separate Bibles for witnesses to swear on in court. Birmingham, Alabama, outlawed interracial checkers games, even in private homes. By custom rather than by law, neighborhoods were divided along strict racial lines; this was just as true up North as it was down South.

World War I shook up the American racial picture in many ways, especially in the North. Adding to a migration that had begun in the mid-1910s, tens of thousands of African-Americans came to work in northern factories that were busily producing war-related products. These African-Americans hoped to find equality and fairer treatment in the North in the postwar years. But when the war ended and the soldiers came home, they were bitterly disappointed. In a terrible white backlash against the rapidly growing African-American presence in the North, rioting broke out in 1919 in 25 cities across the country. These were the bloodiest race riots in American history. As in the Atlanta riot of 1906, nearly all of the violence was done by whites to African-Americans. The Chicago riot was the worst. Mobs took over that city for several days, beating, robbing, and looting. A total of 70 African-Americans were killed in all of the riots. Some died wearing the military uniforms in which they had served their country.

The riots of 1919 had a direct impact on baseball. Throughout the dead-ball era of the 1900s and 1910s, organized baseball remained the same Jim Crow institution that it had become in the 1890s. Nothing much had changed for most African-American ballplayers since the days of Cap Anson. They stayed away from organized leagues and clubs, played challenge matches against each other and off-season exhibitions against white clubs, and held an informal world championship series each Fall. While they were playing in or organizing events like these, however, veteran African-American baseball players like Rube Foster and Sol White continued to dream of a time when, some day soon, the pendulum would swing back and African-Americans could once again cross baseball's color line and compete in organized baseball.

The year 1919 changed all that. The riots forced White and Foster to realize that Jim Crow was here to stay for a long while. African-American baseball needed to develop its own stable leagues in order to survive the long wait until the next thaw in American race relations. Rube Foster summed it up in a phrase that he made into his personal motto: "We have to be ready when the time comes for integration." In 1920 Foster organized eight midwestern African-American

93

*In 1920, Andrew "Rube" Foster organized the
Negro National League, which included his
own team, the Chicago American Giants.*

teams into the Negro National League (NNL). These were the Chicago American Giants, Chicago Giants, (Western) Cuban Stars, Dayton Marcos, Detroit Stars, Indianapolis ABC's, Kansas City Monarchs, and St. Louis Giants. The league recruited most of the great stars of the day, including outfielder Oscar Charleston, pitcher-turned-shortstop Jose Mendez, pitcher "Smokey Joe" Williams, catcher Raleigh "Biz" Mackey, and pitcher John Donaldson. Foster's own club, the powerhouse Chicago American Giants, won the NNL's first pennant.

The NNL was a financial success, often drawing major-league-sized Sunday afternoon crowds of 8,000 in the larger cities. In 1923 a second Negro League was born, the Eastern Colored League (ECL), made up of the Brooklyn Royal Giants, Lincoln Giants, Bacharach Giants, Baltimore Black Sox, Hilldale Club, and (Eastern) Cuban Stars. Hilldale won the ECL's inaugural pennant. In 1906 Rube Foster's old friend Sol White had published *Sol White's History of Colored Baseball,* an invaluable record of the players and teams of early African-American baseball history. White played, managed, and taught baseball during the bleak dead-ball days. Once Foster and White succeeded in 1920 in getting the first stable African-American leagues off the ground, White contributed as a coach, front office executive, and scout for a number of ECL and NNL clubs. Now that there were, in effect, two African-American major leagues, professional baseball was a perfect mirror of American society as a whole. There was one baseball world for whites and another, parallel but completely separate, for African-Americans.

Although many white baseball men—New York Giants manager John McGraw was a prominent example—felt that racial segregation in baseball was wrong, organized baseball's leaders had little to say about race in the 1920s. Commissioner Landis often stuck up for the oppressed major- and minor-league players against the owners, but his sympathy did not extend to African-Americans. As long as he remained in office, not only was the color line strictly observed, but Landis fined or reprimanded anyone in the game who even dared to talk publicly about the subject. Landis was shrewd enough to enforce the owners' Jim Crow policy without ever saying anything about the topic himself. Incredibly, when confronted about the color line in baseball, Landis consistently denied that there was such a thing. As late as 1942, for example, after Dodgers manager Leo Durocher was reported as saying that there were "about a million" Negro Leaguers who could play in the majors if it were not for the color line, Landis called him on the carpet of his Chicago office and convinced him that he had been misquoted. "There is no rule," Landis said, "formal or informal, or any understanding—unwritten, subterranean, or sub-anything—against the hiring of Negro players by the teams of organized baseball." At this time, of course, no African-American had appeared in organized baseball at any level for 43 years.

Landis's statement is especially absurd when you consider that the 1920s were the heyday of the Negro Leagues, a time that produced dozens of the biggest African-American stars of any era. Some of the greatest were:

Pitcher Smokey Joe Williams, a tall right-handed Texan with a legendary fastball. Spotted in San Antonio by Rube Foster, Williams played for the American Giants, the Lincoln Giants, and other top African-American teams between 1912 and 1928. It is difficult to evaluate early Negro League stars like Williams because record-keeping was haphazard at best in the leagues and on the clubs that they played for, but we do know that Williams enjoyed particular success in interracial exhibition contests. He won 22 and lost only 7 against major-league opponents, forcing even an avowed racist like Ty Cobb to admit that he would have been a "sure 30-game-winner" in the white big leagues.

Outfielder, first baseman, and later manager Oscar Charleston, who starred with the famous Pittsburgh Crawfords and over a dozen other Negro League clubs during his 40 seasons in professional baseball. Often compared to Ty Cobb, Charleston was an all-around hitter with power and an aggressive, spikes-up style of base running. A favorite of New York Giants manager John McGraw, Charleston was the key object of McGraw's abortive plot to send several African-American stars to Cuba, arrange their immigration into the U.S., and sign them to play in the white major leagues under false names. In 1921, his greatest season, Charleston led the NNL in batting at .446, home runs with 14, triples with 10, and stolen bases with 28; he put up these numbers in only a 50-game schedule.

Cuban outfielder Cristobal Torriente, one of several Latin American stars to be relegated to the Negro Leagues because of African features. Torriente batted left, hit with power, and played a superb center field. A lifetime .352 hitter in the Cuban Winter League, he batted .396 for the NNL American Giants in 1920 and sparked Foster's club to three straight pennants in 1920, 1921, and 1922.

Pop Lloyd protégé Judy Johnson, the top defensive third baseman in the Negro Leagues of the 1920s. Johnson was a dependable .300 hitter who batted .334 in his Winter ball career in Cuba and .401 in 1929, his best single season, for ECL Hilldale. Johnson was admired and coveted as a player by Connie Mack; after his playing days were over, Johnson worked as a coach and scout for the AL Philadelphia Athletics from 1959 to 1973. He had a terrific eye for baseball talent and was responsible for signing both Negro League superstar Josh Gibson and NL slugger Richie Allen.

Catching great Biz Mackey. Mackey was the finest Negro League defensive catcher in the 1920s; blessed with a powerful right arm, Mackey used the crouching throw that has been popularized by the Tony Penas, Ivan Rodriguezes, and Benito Santiagos of today's game. A top power-hitter as well, Mackey starred with the ECL Hilldale dynasty and batted over .320 for the decade of the 1920s. Mackey was also a great teacher; he groomed future major-league stars Roy Campanella, Larry Doby, Don Newcombe, and Monte Irvin.

Ultra-utility man Martin Dihigo. A great pitcher in Winter ball in Mexico, the Dominican Republic, and his native Cuba, Dihigo played almost every position on the diamond in his 14-year career in the Negro Leagues; as a stunt, he would often do so in the course of a single game. Fast, rifle-armed, and powerful, he regularly batted over .330 and led the ECL or NNL in home runs.

Outfielder and stolen-base king James "Cool Papa" Bell. A repeat .400 hitter and the greatest base runner in Negro League history, Bell played with most of the top Negro League clubs of his day, including the St. Louis Stars, Pittsburgh Crawfords, Homestead Grays, and Kansas City Monarchs. His speed remains the stuff of myth, kept alive by famous tall tales such as the claim that he could turn out the light switch in his room and be in bed before it got dark or that he once slid into second and was hit by his own grounder up the middle.

Going back to baseball's earliest beginnings in the mid-19th century, there had always been plenty of good and even great African-American players who were unknown outside the small world of African-American baseball. But like a few African-American celebrities in music or show business, some outstanding Negro League stars of the 1920s became so famous that they transcended racial boundaries. Many were openly compared to the greatest white stars. Oscar Charleston was called "The Black Ty Cobb" by the white press;

Speedster James "Cool Papa" Bell was one of the many Negro League stars who were prevented by baseball's color line from playing in the white major leagues.

Judy Johnson was called "The Black Pie Traynor." The best example of this is shortstop John "Pop" Lloyd, one of the finest African-American ballplayers of the 1910s and 1920s. He may never have played a game in white, so-called organized baseball, but that did not prevent many white fans and most white reporters and players from knowing about him. Known as "The Black Honus Wagner" in North America and "La Cuchara" in Cuba, (for his skill at scooping ground balls out of the infield dirt), the left-hand-batting and right-hand-throwing Lloyd was a frequent .400 hitter and an amazing fielder at shortstop. He was also incredibly durable; moving to first base to rest his legs around 1920, Lloyd continued to play professional baseball on one level or another until he was almost 60 years old. In his prime he starred for many of the top African-American independent clubs, including the Cuban X-Giants, the Philadelphia Giants, and the Leland Giants. Playing with New York's Lincoln Giants in 1913, Lloyd led his team to a 9-2 drubbing of Pete Alexander and the NL Philadelphia Phillies in an exhibition match. After the advent of the Negro Leagues, Lloyd served as first baseman/manager for several Negro League clubs. When he retired from baseball for good, Lloyd remained a popular figure on both sides of the color line. A great friend to children, he served as Little League commissioner of Atlantic City, New Jersey, during the 1940s. In 1949 the city named its new ballpark after him. When someone asked the real Honus Wagner, who was probably the best all-around player in major-league history after Babe Ruth, what he thought about Lloyd's nickname, he answered: "I am honored to have John Lloyd called the Black Wagner. It is my privilege to have been compared with him."

The better African-American stars like Lloyd played, the harder it was to explain why there was no place in the major leagues—not to mention the minors—for African-American stars of this caliber. In the early 1930s, white baseball officials became increasingly defensive about the color line. In response to criticism

Babe Ruth, Honus Wagner, and other baseball greats considered shortstop John Henry "Pop" Lloyd the best player they ever saw. Lloyd never played a game in the white major leagues.

from the press NL President John Heydler repeated the party line that there was no color line. "I do not recall one instance," he said, "where baseball has allowed either race, creed, or color to enter into its selection of players." African-Americans, he said, were simply not good enough to play in white baseball. However, because in many major-league cities Negro League teams rented white teams' ballparks while they were on the road, millions of white fans could buy a ticket to a Negro League game and see for themselves that this was not true.

THE YEAR: 1924

The New York Giants won their fourth flag in four years. The Yankees, however, failed to defend their championship of 1923 and fell to two games behind the underdog Washington Senators, who had finished 23½ games out the year before. Nobody could blame Ruth; he won his only career batting title at .378 and led in the usual categories: homers with 46, runs with 143, walks with 142, on-base average, and slugging average. The Yankees pitching faltered a bit, compiling an ERA of 3.86, second in the league, as Joe Bush's 17–16 record and Bob Shawkey's 4.11 ERA offset better efforts from 21-game winners Pennock, Waite Hoyt, and Sam Jones. The deciding factor in the 1924 AL race, however, was the terrific pitching of Walter Johnson, who for the first time in his 19-year career played on a team that provided him with a reasonable amount of offensive and defensive support.

The 36-year-old fastballer led the AL in strikeouts with 158, wins with 23, shutouts with six, and ERA at 2.72. He was voted AL MVP; again, Eddie Collins finished second for last-place Chicago. Rounding out the rest of Washington's staff, which led the AL in ERA at 3.35, was lefty Tom Zachary, who went 15–9 with a

2.75 ERA, 16–11 George Mogridge, and early relief ace Fred "Firpo" Marberry, who won 11 games and would have recorded 15 saves using modern scoring rules. The Senators' offense achieved mediocrity thanks to outfielder Leon "Goose" Goslin, who hit .344 with a league-leading 129 RBIs; Sam Rice, who hit .334 and scored 106 runs; and first baseman Joe Judge, who batted .324.

Brooklyn was a surprise contender in the NL race, sparked by hitting stars Jack Fournier, who was second in the NL in RBIs with 116 and first in home runs with 27, and Zach Wheat, who hit .375, second only to Rogers Hornsby's .424—the highest batting mark of the century. Brooklyn also got solid years from spitballer Burleigh Grimes and Clarence "Dazzy" Vance, who combined for 50 wins, 60 complete games, and 620 innings; they finished first and second in almost every pitching category. For the first time, an MVP was chosen in the National League and the winner was Vance, who won the NL ERA title as well at 2.16. With a league-leading 121 runs, 227 hits, 373 total bases, and 89 walks, Hornsby turned in his finest season for sixth-place St. Louis, but it was the New York Giants who led the NL in runs scored behind Frisch, Youngs, and George Kelly, who batted .324 and drove in an NL-high 136 runs. McGraw's team beat back challenges from Brooklyn, which finished 1½ games back at 92–62, and Pittsburgh, which came in three games off the pace at 90–63.

The Giants and Senators played a seven-game series that was one of the closest in history. Four of the games were decided by one run and two went into extra innings; the teams' statistical summaries are virtually indistinguishable. Washington came out on top in a 12-inning seventh game that was decided by two bad-hop hits over third baseman Freddy Lindstrom's head and comical misplays by New York catcher Hank

Gowdy and shortstop Travis Jackson. Walter Johnson got the win in relief, his first career World Series victory.

A wild card in the racial situation of the 1910s and 1920s was the new Caribbean influence in baseball caused by the twin phenomena of white players playing Winter baseball and Cuban ballplayers playing in the major leagues. Baseball had a long history in Cuba going back to the 1870s, but it flourished during the time of American domination of Cuba from 1901 to 1934. During this time, the U.S. frequently sent troops to Cuba to protect American interests, without formally taking possession of the former Spanish colony. This led to increased contact and trade between the two countries. To white baseball men like Reds manager and later Washington Senators manager and owner Clark Griffith, the Cuba of the 1910s and 1920s represented a treasure trove of unexploited playing talent. To others, the island represented a danger to the baseball color line and American racial values. The problem was that Cuba, like most Caribbean nations, had a more racially mixed society and a much more liberal attitude toward race than America. Racism American-style and Jim Crow made little sense in a country where members of the same family might range in skin color from dark brown to white.

The new Cuban influence took two forms. One was the relatively new practice of American major-league teams traveling to Cuba after the season for Winter barnstorming tours against local teams. Since it was off-season for African-American clubs, too, Cuban teams were often stocked with African-American players who had come down from the United States to earn an extra paycheck. Sometimes these teams held their own or even beat the white major leaguers. Going back to the late 1880s, organized baseball had been uneasy about its teams, particularly championship teams, playing postseason exhibition games against African-Americans. In 1887 the (entirely African-American) Cuban Giants had barely lost to the world champion Detroit Wolverines by a margin of 6-4, after going into the eighth leading 4-2. This was too close for comfort for organized baseball, which first discouraged and then later outlawed such games. A 1909 trip to Cuba by another Detroit team, the AL champion Tigers, did not help matters. A year after Cuban teams with African-Americans had beaten Frank Bancroft's Cincinnati Reds in 7 games out of 11, the 1909 Tigers compiled an equally dismal 4–8 record on their trip. One of the Tigers' losses came in the form of a ten-inning no-hitter by Eustaquio Pedroza. Even though they were missing Wahoo Sam Crawford and Ty Cobb, the team's two biggest stars, the Tigers were embarrassed and angry. They returned the following Fall with Crawford, looking for revenge. Their record stood at 3–3–1, including another no-hitter by Pedroza, when they called in the cavalry: Ty Cobb, who was vacationing on the mainland.

Cobb's arrival turned the series around; he batted .370 and sparked the Tigers to four wins in their final five games. But this time it was Cobb who was angry. In his first game Cobb was thrown out stealing three times out of three by African-American catcher Bruce Petway; when he tried his famous hook slide into second base, shortstop Pop Lloyd slipped a leg under him and flipped him into the outfield. An unabashed racist, Cobb was also embarrassed that he had been shut down by Jose Mendez, the dark Cuban ace, and outhit by three African-Americans. Against the Tigers' big-league pitching, Lloyd hit .500, Grant Johnson hit .412, and Petway hit .390. Cobb publicly swore that he would never play against African-Americans again. It was a vow that he kept for the rest of his 24-year career in baseball.

All told, American major-league teams played 65 games against Cuban teams during the 1900s and early

1910s, nearly all of which included African-Americans or Cubans considered too dark-skinned to cross the organized baseball color line. While it is true that not every American team brought along every one of its starting players, half of them were pennant winners or World Series champions. Through 1911 the record of American major-league teams in Cuba stood at 32 wins, 32 losses, and one tie. After the 1911 Athletics went 1–5 on their trip to Cuba, AL President Ban Johnson put an end to all Cuban barnstorming by AL clubs. He made no secret about the reason: "We want no makeshift clubs calling themselves the A's to go to Cuba to be beaten by colored teams." In the 1920s Commissioner Kenesaw Mountain Landis extended the ban to both major leagues.

The other way Cubans influenced organized baseball was by coming to play in the United States as individuals. The first to make the trip were outfielder Armando Marsans and third baseman Rafael Almeida, both light-skinned and both signed in 1911 to play for the Reds. Thanks to Reds business manager Frank Bancroft—who enjoyed close relations with Cuban baseball men going back to 1879, when he had been the first manager to bring a major-league club to Cuba—the Reds and their manager Clark Griffith had first pick of Cuban talent. Many in baseball were alarmed. They felt that this would open the door to Cuban players with more dubious racial backgrounds and undermine the color line. Among African-Americans, their arrival was greeted with great joy and hope for the same reason.

The "Cuban question" was solved by an unspoken compromise. Marsans and Almeida were allowed to stay in organized baseball, but not without going through an insulting charade intended to discourage teams from signing Cubans with the slightest suggestion of African features. Griffith sent to Cuba for the family histories of the two players going all the way back to Spain; he then announced in the newspapers that he could document that Marsans and Almeida were "two of the purest bars of Castilian soap ever floated to these shores." Other Cubans followed, including pitching great Adolfo "Dolf" Luque, who won 194 games and two ERA titles in 20 big-league seasons between 1914 and 1935. Later Cuban and other Hispanic players were divided into two groups; the lighter-skinned players were allowed to cross the color line and the darker-skinned players were forced to stay at home or play in the Negro Leagues. One example was Puerto Rican slugger Perucho Cepeda, who grew bitter watching less talented Hispanic players cross the baseball color line while he was held back by his dark skin; a generation later, Cepeda's son Orlando gave major-league fans a hint of what they had missed, batting .297, hitting 379 home runs, and starring in three World Series with the Giants and the Cardinals between 1958 and 1974.

After Luque, Griffith went on to import dozens more Cubans to play for the Senators, which he managed from 1912 to 1920. None of these was obviously of African descent, although many major-league owners continued to fear that the signing of Cubans and other Hispanics would weaken the color line. According to one observer at a major-league owners meeting from the mid-1940s where Branch Rickey's plan to break the color line by signing African-American infielder Jackie Robinson was discussed, Clark Griffith took a firm stand against signing any "niggers." "But Clark," Rickey replied icily, "you already have."

THE YEAR: 1925

The New York Yankees found out just how dependent they really were on Babe Ruth in 1925, when their overweight and worn down right fielder lost two months of the season to a mystery ailment that may or may not have been related to his celebrated overeating. Surgery and a suspension levied by manager Miller Huggins for off-field misbehavior limited his season to 98 games and the Yankees collapsed to seventh place and a 69–85 record. The good news for New York was that they seized this opportunity to rebuild an aging team, bringing in, among others, rookie first baseman Lou Gehrig. With Ruth, Gehrig would later form the foundation of the famous "Murderers' Row" club of 1927. Ironically, Gehrig started his famous consecutive-game streak on June 1, less than a month after Yankee teammate Everett Scott's record 1,307-game streak came to an end. Scott had played shortstop every day from June 20, 1916, to May 5, 1925.

Washington shocked the baseball world a second time by repeating in 1925. The Senators won 96 games to come in 8½ games ahead of a rebuilding Philadel-phia A's team that featured young slugger Al Simmons and rookies Gordon "Mickey" Cochrane and Robert "Lefty" Grove. Philadelphia's Eddie Rommel tied the White Sox' Ted Lyons for the AL lead in wins with 21. The Senators were a running team; Sam Rice and Goose Goslin were tied for second in stolen bases with 26 apiece and Goslin hit a league-leading 20 triples; Rice and Goslin also scored a combined 227 runs and drove in 200. The AL MVP was former Yankee shortstop Roger Peckinpaugh, who batted .294 and formed, with 28 year-old player/manager Stanley "Bucky" Harris, Washington's double-play combo. The Big Train, now 37 years old, slipped slightly to 20–7 with a 3.07 ERA; A's rookie Lefty Grove surpassed him in strikeouts, 116-108. Slugging Yankee outfielder Bob Meusel led the league in home runs with 33, and Detroit's Harry Heilmann beat out Tris Speaker for the batting title on the final day of the season, .393 to .389, after an excit-ing September charge.

In the NL, the Cincinnati Reds dominated nearly every pitching category and compiled a league-low 3.38 team ERA, an amazing accomplishment for the 1920s' biggest run-scoring year. Eppa Rixey and Pete Donohue each won 21 games, and Donohue, Rixey, and Cuban star Dolf Luque combined for 879 innings pitched. The trio was also one, two, and four in ERA at 2.63 for Luque, 2.88 for Rixey, and 3.07 for Donohue. But it was Pittsburgh's bats that made the big noise in 1925, as the Pirates won their first pennant since 1909 and became the first NL team ever to score 900 runs on the strength of Hazen "Kiki" Cuyler's league-leading 144 runs and 26 triples (pronounced "Kai-Kai", Cuyler's nickname was a cruel reference to his habit of stuttering), Max Carey's NL-high 46 stolen bases, and third baseman Harold "Pie" Traynor's .320 batting average. Rogers Hornsby batted .403 and won a second Triple Crown but his team, the Cardinals, finished 18 games out of the money.

The Pirates won a seven-game World Series that was the flip side of the 1924 series. Walter Johnson began the series 2–0, only to lose the deciding contest 9-7, and Peckinpaugh was the fielding goat with eight errors at short. One of the few Senators highlights was Sam Rice's circus catch of Earl Smith's game-three drive into the right-field stands.

The baseball color line may have withstood the strain caused by the Cuban question, but the forces of racism and Jim Crow were not able to stop all contact between the races. In spite of the disapproval of the major-league baseball establishment, interracial baseball exhibition games and barnstorming match-ups continued in various forms as they had in the 1880s and 1890s. The main reason for this was simple: race sells. As in boxing today, sports fans of the 1910s and 1920s were intrigued by contests that pitted top white clubs against the best African-American competition. Such matches were eagerly attended by fans of both races until the mid-1920s, when Commissioner Kenesaw Mountain Landis banned all interracial barnstorming by intact major-league teams. Landis's edict, however, failed to prevent African-American teams from playing exhibitions against so-called "all-star" teams made up of white players from different major league clubs. The reason that these games were so hard to stop was that they were so profitable for the players. In 1947, for example, St. Louis Cardinals star Stan Musial caused a stir when he complained that his share of that year's World Series money came to less than half of the $10,000 paycheck he made from one barnstorming tour with African-American superstar Satchel Paige.

Jim Crow and the color line were also unable to prevent white and African-American baseball players, executives, and owners from having friendships, business dealings, and even teacher-pupil relationships out of the public eye. Starting with the Athletics in 1906 and the Yankees in 1907, major-league teams began to rent their ballparks to African-American teams. In the 1920s, ballpark rentals to Negro League teams became an important revenue source for major-league clubs. Other business dealings inevitably followed. In addition to his relationship with Anson, Rube Foster was friendly with AL President Ban Johnson and White Sox owner Charlie Comiskey during the 1910s. Athletics owner/ manager Connie Mack had ties to the African-American baseball community in Philadelphia. John McGraw hired Rube Foster as a non-uniformed pitching coach; Foster was believed to have taught Hall of Famer Christy Mathewson his famous "fadeaway," or screwball, pitch. Rumor also had it that the great Cubs catcher Johnny Kling was taught his trademark crouch-and-throw by African-American star Bruce Petway. By 1930, the racial situation in baseball was much like that in popular music where bands, nightclubs, and record companies maintained a strict separation in public between African-Americans and whites. Off-stage it was a different story. In music and in baseball, for public consumption the races lived in two separate worlds. Behind the scenes, however, musicians and ballplayers on both sides of the color line knew, respected, and learned from each other.

CHAPTER SEVEN

Murderers' Row: The First New York Yankees Dynasty

Babe Ruth had made comebacks before, but after the disastrous 1925 season, many doubted that he could do it again. Despite his poor season, the suspension by Miller Huggins, and all the embarrassing publicity about his private life and his failing marriage, Ruth had done nothing to improve his chances of being named Husband of the Year. Helen Ruth gave up on him and returned to Boston to stay; Claire Hodgson stood by Ruth, but she knew enough not to expect him to be faithful. Babe Ruth's sex life had become stand-up comedy material. Humorist Will Rogers joked: "You girls certainly got to get up early in the morning if you want to marry Babe Ruth." At the New York sportswriters' dinner, a writer dressed up as Miller Huggins sang the following parody of a popular song, written by fellow writer Bill Slocum:

> I wonder where my Babe Ruth is tonight?
> He grabbed his hat and coat and ducked
>   from sight.

I wonder where he'll be
At half past two or three?
He may be at a dance or in a fight.
He may be at some cozy roadside inn.
He may be drinking tea or maybe—gin.
I know he's with a dame,
I wonder what's her name?
I wonder where my Babe Ruth is tonight?[1]

Ruth, who was at the dinner, laughed as hard as anybody.

If Babe Ruth could not help himself where women were concerned, however, he resolved to take control of his life in other ways. "I've been a sap," he told an interviewer, "I have to face the facts. No more of the good-time Charlie business for me. I am going to start all over, and I hope they'll be watching my smoke in 1926." He was serious about getting back in shape. Instead of his usual regimen of banquets, parties, and trips to the West Coast, Ruth spent the off-season of 1925–26 working off 20 or 30 pounds at McGovern's gym in New York. He reported to spring training at a muscular 212 pounds, his lowest weight in at least five years.

Ruth's mood going into the 1926 season paralleled that of his Yankees teammates, who were collectively embarrassed by 1925 and determined to change things in 1926. General manager Ed Barrow and scout Paul Krichell had rebuilt the Yankees line-up, getting rid of players like Whitey Witt, Wally Schang, Everret Scott, and Wally Pipp, who were on the down side of their careers, and bringing in talented youngsters like Columbia college star Lou Gehrig, Tony Lazzeri, Mark Koenig, and Benny Bengough. This younger, leaner, more determined Yankees team clicked in spring training and roared into first place by early May. After surviving a late-season scare from Tris Speaker's tenacious

113

Cleveland Indians, the New Yorkers won the AL pennant by three games. Ruth hit .372 with 47 homers and 145 RBIs; Gehrig and Lazzeri combined for 34 more home runs and 221 RBIs. Pitching mainstays Herb Pennock, Urban Shocker, and Waite Hoyt went a combined 58–34. Even though the Yankees lost a thrilling, seven-game World Series to the St. Louis Cardinals, there was a general feeling that this was only the beginning. "Hug and I both knew," Ed Barrow writes in his 1951 autobiography, "that the team we had remodeled and resurrected from the shambles of 1925 was a good one, and, with that hard season to temper it, would be a better one."

THE YEAR: 1926

Under new player/manager Rogers Hornsby, who had replaced Branch Rickey when Rickey was kicked upstairs 38 games into the 1925 season, the Cardinals brought St. Louis that city's first pennant in half a century of National League competition. It was the first St. Louis championship of any kind since the old St. Louis Browns of Charles Comiskey and Arlie Latham won their final AA pennant in 1888. Distracted by his managerial responsibilities, Hornsby slipped to a .317 batting mark with 11 home runs, 96 runs, and 93 RBIs; still, his team scored a league-leading 817 runs. First baseman "Sunny Jim" Bottomley led the NL in doubles with 40 and RBIs with 120, third baseman Les Bell drove in 100 runs and hit .325, and MVP catcher Bob O'Farrell hit .293 with 30 doubles and seven homers. Hornsby put together a durable starting rotation of Flint Rhem, who tied for the league lead in wins with 20; 16–12 Bill Sherdel; and veteran Jesse Haines, who went 13–4 with a 3.25 ERA. Cardinals pitchers threw an NL-high 90 complete games; 39-year-old ex-Cub Pete Alexander went 9–7 in a relief/spot-starting role. Cincinnati came in second by two games on the strength of good years from catcher Eugene "Bubbles" Hargrave, who won the batting title at .353; .323-hitting Edd Roush; and pitchers Pete Donohue, who won 20 games, and Carl Mays, who went 19–12 with a 3.14 ERA. Pittsburgh was less than the sum of its parts, finishing third in spite of rookie Paul Waner's NL-high 22 triples and .336 batting average; Kiki Cuyler's league-leading 113 runs; and 20-win performances from ace Ray Kremer, who took the ERA title at 2.61, and veteran righty Lee Meadows.

The Yankees returned to the top with a 91–63 record; the team barely survived blowing most of a ten-game lead in September. The great Walter Johnson finally got old, going 15–16 in his last full year as a starting pitcher, and the rest of the Senators staff collapsed around him. Rice and Goslin were true to form, batting .337 and .354, respectively, and scoring 203 runs, with 58 doubles and 29 triples between them. Veteran first baseman George Burns hit 64 doubles, the second-best seasonal total in history, for Cleveland, along with 114 RBIs and a .358 batting average; he won the AL MVP. New shortstop Mark Koenig solidified the Yankees defense and the big three of the New York line-up—Ruth, Gehrig, and up-and-coming slugger Earle Combs—all had big years. Ruth hit .372, second only to Detroit's Heinie Manush at .378, scored a league-leading 139 runs, and drove in an AL-high 145; he also led in walks with 144, home runs with 47, on-base average at .516, and slugging average at .737. A blossoming Gehrig led all AL hitters in triples with 20, scored 135 runs, and banged out 47 doubles. Combs hit his usual .299 with 12 triples and 113 runs. Philadelphia had the AL's best pitching staff, including ERA-leader Lefty Grove at 2.51, 12–4 junkballer Howard Ehmke, fastballer Rube Walberg, and knuckleballer Eddie Rommel, who was fourth in ERA at 3.08.

The two main hitmen of Murderers' Row, Lou Gehrig and Babe Ruth, pose before a game.

Despite Babe Ruth's four home run-performance, which included an unprecedented three in one game, the World Series went the full seven games and was decided when the grizzled Pete Alexander, who had already beaten the Yankees with complete-game efforts in games two and six, came out of the bullpen to protect Jesse Haines's 3-2 lead in the seventh. He struck out rookie second baseman Tony Lazzeri with the bases loaded and two out, and then held New York down until he walked Babe Ruth with two outs in the ninth. A frustrated Ruth, who was walked 11 times by St. Louis pitchers, tried to steal second and put himself into scoring position, but was gunned down by O'Farrell to end the game and the series.

The 1927 New York Yankees have gone down as the greatest baseball team in the history of the major leagues. Certainly, it is no easy task to argue against that proposition. Propelled by an underrated pitching staff and "Murderers' Row," as their awesome line-up was nicknamed, the Yankees led in the AL standings every single day of the season, a feat that has only been duplicated once, by the 1984 Detroit Tigers. They won 110 games, finished a record 19 games ahead of second-place Cleveland, and clinched the AL flag by Labor Day—earlier than any pennant-winner in modern major-league history. Like most great teams, the Yankees never let up or showed any mercy to also-rans; their record against seventh-place St. Louis was 21–1, the Browns' lone win coming in their last game against New York. The 1927 Yankees were a great slugging team, but they were more versatile than most home-run hitting clubs. The team had a solid defense; stole 90 bases, tied for fifth in the AL; and featured a splendid pitching staff of Hoyt, Pennock, Shocker, Dutch Ruether, and relief sensation Wilcy Moore that dominated opposing hitters almost as completely as the Murderers' Row did opposing pitchers.

What the 1927 Yankees will always be remembered for, of course, is power. The team batted .307 with a league-leading 158 homers, 103 triples, and 975 runs scored to outclass the rest of the AL the way Ruth himself had done in 1920 and 1921. Their 158 homers rep-

117

resent an incredible 36 percent of the league total; the nearest team, the Philadelphia A's, hit only 56. Today, nearly every team has at least one or two good power hitters. In 1927 New York had a virtual monopoly on the long ball; three of the eight AL hitters who reached double figures in homers wore pinstripes and the pair of Ruth and Gehrig hit 51 more than any other whole team. To an opposing pitcher, the New York line-up was something out of a nightmare: lead-off man and out-fielder Earle Combs, who batted .356 and scored 137 runs; shortstop Mark Koenig, who batted .285; Ruth; first baseman Gehrig, who batted .373 with 47 homers and 175 RBIs; outfielder Bob Meusel, who hit .337 with eight homers; second baseman Tony Lazzeri, who hit .309 with 18 homers; third baseman Joe Dugan, who hit .269, and catcher Pat Collins, who hit .275 with seven home runs. During the 1927 season Joe Dugan described what it was like to be the least intimidating member of a line-up like this. "It's always the same," Dugan said, "Combs walks. Koenig singles. Ruth hits one out of the park. Gehrig doubles. Lazzeri triples. Then Dugan goes in the dirt on his can."

Going into the 1927 season, Jacob Ruppert said he had a feeling that Babe Ruth was "ready to have his greatest year." The 72,000 fans who crammed into Yankee Stadium on Opening Day must have had the same feeling. They saw the Yanks defeat Philadelphia, 8-3. The Yankees then took 23 of its first 33 games, including 10 out of 13 on a long western road trip. In July, sportswriter John Kieran wrote: "It isn't a race in the American League, it's a landslide." The team never took its foot off the gas pedal. Coming into a July Fourth double header with Washington and an 11½ game lead, the Yankees swept by a combined score of 30–2. They tied the AL record of 106 wins on September 24; their season total of 110 wins set a record that stood until 1954.

Third baseman Joe Dugan often joked about his status as the least frightening hitter in the Yankees Murderers' Row.

The 1927 Yankees won ballgames in every conceivable way, but their specialty was dramatic comebacks. The expression "five o'clock thunder" was coined that year to refer to the dependability of Ruth and Co.'s late-inning bursts of four, five, or six runs, which seemed to come whenever they were needed. Sportswriter Paul Gallico tells what it was like to watch Murderers' Row doing its thing:

I used to sit in the press box with my heart in my throat, my palms sweaty, my mouth all dry and cottony, and my nerves prickly and on edge, watching the Yankees play. It was like when I was a kid and there used to be a lot of blasting going on down on Park Avenue where they were digging the cut for the New York Central tracks. There would be a laborer with a box with a plunger handle and they would spread the mats and get ready to dynamite. There would be a nerve-racking suspense and what seemed like an interminable wait. But then there would go one hell of a big boom and chunks of Park Avenue would go flying through the air. Well, it was just like that with the 1927 Yankees. You never knew when the batting order was going to push the handle down . . . and the Yankees would be legging it over the plate with runs, sometimes in single file but more often in bunches of twos and threes as home runs cleared the bases."[2]

THE YEAR: 1927

The year 1927 opened with an unpleasant reminder of baseball's corrupt pre-Ruthian past, when ex-pitcher Dutch Leonard accused all-time greats Ty Cobb and Tris Speaker of fixing a 1919 game between Detroit and Cleveland. Despite two incriminating letters produced by Leonard, Commissioner Landis permitted the pair to resign from their clubs without any official finding of guilt or innocence; both signed as player/managers with new AL teams for 1927, Cobb with Philadelphia and Speaker with Washington. This mini-scandal resulted in the firing of Ban Johnson from the AL presidency after 27 years of service, when he annoyed Landis by publicly protesting that his decision had smeared the two baseball legends without proof.

The public's attention was soon diverted, however, by the heroics of the 1927 Yankees, the best Yankees team ever, who came in well ahead of a good Philadelphia team sparked by a comeback from the 40 year-old Cobb, who hit .357. Babe Ruth hit more home runs than any other single team, and led in on-base average at .487. His sidekick Gehrig finished second in the AL with 47. Ruth slugged .772 and Gehrig .765, both marks surpassed in history only by Ruth's 1920 and 1921 seasons, and between them Ruth and Gehrig accounted for almost 25 percent of the league's home runs. Ruth was first in runs with 158, nine more than Gehrig, and second in RBIs, with 164 to his teammate's 175; if Ruth had batted fourth and Gehrig third, these numbers could have been reversed. Because of the custom, left over from the Chalmers days, that held that a man should not be voted MVP twice in his career, Gehrig won the AL award over Detroit's Harry Heilmann, who hit .398 and won the batting title to become the only non-Yankee to lead the AL in a major offensive statistic.

All this slugging overshadowed the Yankees pitching, which allowed a league-low 599 runs and compiled the AL's best ERA at 3.20. Waite Hoyt led in wins with 22, Wilcy Moore, Hoyt, and Shocker were first, second, and fourth in ERA at 2.28, 2.63, and 2.84, respectively, and four Yankees topped .700 in winning percentage. As a staff, New York also led the AL in fewest hits, fewest walks, and most shutouts.

In the NL, Pittsburgh won a squeaker over the Cardinals and the Giants; the three teams were separated in the final standings by only two games. The

121

Pirates' Paul Waner won the batting title at .380 and led in RBIs with 131, hits with 237, and triples with 17; his younger brother Lloyd led in runs with 133 and was third in batting at .355. Fired as manager and traded from St. Louis to New York, Hornsby rebounded to hit .361, second in the NL, with 26 home runs and 125 RBIs. The fourth-place Cubs featured home-run co-leader Hack Wilson and pitcher Charlie Root, who led in wins with 26 and innings pitched with 309; Pittsburgh's Ray Kremer won the ERA title at 2.47. Forty-year-old Pete Alexander mounted a comeback with the Cardinals to go 21–10 with the NL's second-best ERA: 2.52.

The World Series took only four days, as New York outscored the Pirates 23-10, outpitched them 2.00 ERA to 5.19, and swept the series in four. Babe Ruth batted .400 with two homers and seven RBIs. The Yankees would not lose another World Series game until 1936— after a streak of 12 consecutive postseason victories.

The team within the 1927 Yankees team was the tandem of Babe Ruth and Lou Gehrig, who launched 60 home runs and 47 home runs, respectively. Ruth was never better than in 1927 and the presence of Gehrig was a large part of the reason. Batting fourth, Gehrig protected Ruth. Despite the fact that Ruth reached his career high in homers in 1927, opposing pitchers were far from eager to pitch around him and face Gehrig, who batted .373 with 52 doubles, 18 triples, and 47 homers. The Babe walked 138 times, a large number except when compared to earlier seasons, when he had been passed as many as 144, 148, or even 170 times. As the only AL hitter besides Lazzeri to break the 20-home-run barrier, Gehrig also provided Ruth with a rival for the AL home-run title. For much of the season, the two sluggers waged an exciting race. Ruth hit four home runs in April, 12 in

Yankees skipper Miller Huggins tried, and usually failed, to control the unruly Ruth.

May, and nine in June; remarkably, Gehrig matched this pace and even passed Ruth briefly in early July. From that point on, however, Gehrig was left in the dust as Babe Ruth hit nine in July, for a total of 34, and another nine in August.

By September, the home-run race was no longer Ruth vs. Gehrig but Ruth vs. Ruth. Despite the fact that it would require Ruth to hit an unheard-of 17 home runs in the final month of the season, the question on everybody's mind was whether he could break his own record of 59, set in 1921. It did not look good; with 14 games to go in the season, Ruth had only 51. He added four to his total in the next ten games to reach 56 with only four games left. He then hit three homers in the next two games to tie his record; he now had two games' worth of chances to hit number 60. Ruth did not keep baseball fans in suspense for too long; with one out in the eighth inning of the second-to-last regular-season game of 1927, Ruth golfed a screwball thrown by lefty Tom Zachary of the Washington Senators deep into the right-field bleachers. "60!," Ruth shouted to his teammates in the clubhouse after the game, "let's see some son of a bitch try to top that one!"

The 1927 season was the high-water mark for the Yankees as a team and for Babe Ruth personally. The Yankees won other pennants and had other dynasties, but they were never better than the competition by as great a margin as they were that year. In the words of one contemporary writer, "If the old Baltimore Orioles are still talked of after thirty years, this team will be talked of for the next century." That prophecy is well on its way to coming true. As for Ruth, the 1927 season raised him to a new, even higher level of adulation and hero-worship. He and Gehrig toured the country with a pair of all-star teams called the "Bustin' Babes" and the "Larrupin' Lous" and played a series of barnstorming games to sell-out crowds; Ruth's share of the receipts came to $70,000, or more than the Yankees paid him for a year's salary. Ruth's fame extended far beyond baseball and his name and image appeared every-where: in magazine ads, on cereal boxes, on the vaudeville stage, and in Hollywood films. His endorsement in the presidential election of 1928 was eagerly sought by both sides; Ruth favored Democrat Al Smith and made newspaper headlines across the country when he refused to pose for a picture with the Republican candidate, Herbert Hoover. In the words of former Red Sox teammate Harry Hooper,

> *I saw it all happen, from beginning to end. But sometimes I still can't believe what I saw: this 19 year-old kid, poorly educated, only lightly brushed by the social veneer we call civilization, gradually transformed into the idol of American youth and the symbol of baseball the world over—a man loved by more people and with an intensity of feeling that perhaps has never been equaled before or since. I saw a man transformed from a human being into something pretty close to a god."*[3]

Babe Ruth would go on to swat 54 homers the following year and win four more home-run titles, but his 60 home runs became, in time, one of baseball's greatest records—a distant, apparently unclimbable peak like Cy Young's 511 wins or Cobb's 4,191 career base hits. Even though it was finally surpassed in 1961 by another Yankee, Roger Maris, the magic of Ruth's number 60 somehow lives on, undiminished. In a way, to have an ordinary ball player like Maris break Ruth's record only reminded the baseball world that the greatness of Babe Ruth transcended mere statistics. As Ruth's buddy Waite Hoyt said, long before 1961:

> *Somebody may come along some day who will hit more than 60 home runs in a season or more than 714 [Ruth's lifetime total] in a career, but*

Pitcher Waite Hoyt provided a dependable arm in the Yankee rotation. Hoyt was Ruth's best friend on the team.

that won't make him another Ruth. . . .[Ruth] was the greatest crowd pleaser of them all! It wasn't so much that he hit homers, it was how he hit them and the circumstances under which he hit them. Another Ruth? Never!"[4]

Quality Out of Quantity: Branch Rickey and the Farm System

For the first quarter of the 20th century, two giants stood head-and-shoulders above the rest of major-league baseball: John McGraw of the New York Giants and Connie Mack of the Philadelphia Athletics. Both had cut their baseball teeth in the 1890s, when baseball was more like a street fight than a sporting event. During the dead-ball era and afterward, both ran their baseball teams with the passion, creativity, and intensity that characterized the national pastime in the glory days of King Kelly, Big Ed Delahanty, and Sliding Billy Hamilton. Other managers and other organizations of the 1900s, 1910s, and 1920s copied their innovations and imitated their style. In the 1920s a new great baseball mind came along who changed baseball as profoundly as McGraw or Mack: an ex-catcher named Wesley Branch Rickey.

Rickey, who went by his middle name, was born in rural Ohio in 1881 and raised in a strict Methodist family. Like fellow Ohioan Ban Johnson, the young Rickey was torn between his obvious athletic talent and his family's desire that he go into a more respectable profession than sports. From 1900 to 1915 Rickey vacillated between baseball and a career in law. He caught for the St. Louis Browns and the New York Highlanders from 1905 to 1907, coached the University of Michigan baseball team, and earned a law degree—after which he almost immediately discovered that he detested practicing law. Rickey could have had a longer major-league career based on his smarts and defensive skills if he had not promised his mother that he would never play baseball on Sunday. For this reason he was cut from the 1904 Reds before getting into a single game by manager Joe Kelley, the hard-bitten old Oriole. Rickey's other problem was that he could not hit; in 119 career games behind the plate he batted .239 with three homers and 39 RBIs. Rickey was hired to manage the Browns in 1913, but had a falling out with new owner Phil Ball in 1915. After serving in the military, Rickey was snapped up by the crosstown Cardinals, where he managed from 1919 to 1925. His career record as a manager was not much better than his stats as a player: 597 wins and 664 losses for a winning percentage of .473.

By the early 1920s, St. Louis owner Sam Breadon was convinced that Rickey's true talents lay in the front office, not on the playing field. In 1925 Breadon hired veteran slugger Rogers Hornsby to manage the Cardinals and put Rickey in charge of the front office. From then on, he flourished. Branch Rickey was a baseball visionary who had a genius for getting the most out of an organization, its coaches, scouts, and ballplayers—and doing so as cheaply as possible. The problem faced by the St. Louis Cardinals and so many other major-league clubs in small markets was that baseball talent was sold to the highest bidder. Because there was no amateur draft, wealthy clubs like the Yankees, Giants, Cubs, and

White Sox hired the most scouts, bought the most minor-leaguers, and signed the best high school and college prospects. Rickey had great contacts in college baseball—this is how he signed George Sisler, for example, out from under the many richer clubs that wanted him—but he soon found that high-quality scouting was not enough. No matter how good the Cardinals scouts were at uncovering talent, they could not afford to pay top dollar and other clubs knew it. In fact, the club's good reputation for scouting worked against it. As soon as St. Louis made an offer to a prospect, the youngster's coach or a friend would telephone one of the wealthier clubs, who would then swoop down and outbid the Cardinals.

Rickey had a plan to change all that. Based on the philosophy of "quality out of quantity," Rickey plotted to get control of as many minor leagues and minor-league franchises as possible. At that time, virtually every minor-league team was independent, run by an owner who signed his own players and sold the better ones to other minor- or major-league clubs or not, as he wished. There was a minor-league draft, under which some minor-league players were available to major-league clubs for a fixed draft price, but cash-starved clubs like St. Louis could not afford to take much advantage of it. If he got control of thousands of players while they were still in the low minors, Rickey reasoned, he would no longer have to worry about being outbid later for the cream of the crop. The final step in his plan would be to set up a pyramid of minor-league subsidiaries, with many clubs in the low minors and fewer in the more competitive higher minor leagues, so that prospects would be coached and scouted in a systematic way. Players would be weeded out as they moved up the pyramid, leaving only the best prospects at the top, ready to step into the Cardinals' line-up.

Starting in 1925, Rickey used Breadon's money to do just that. He bought interests in a Class D (the equivalent of today's Class A, or extremely low minors) outfit in Fort Smith, Arkansas, and in the Class A (today's AA) Houston Buffaloes of the competitive Texas State League. In 1927 he bought the AA (then the top minor-league classification, the equivalent of today's AAA) Syracuse, New York, club and moved it to Rochester, New York. By 1928, Rickey controlled five of the 18 so-called "farm clubs," or minor-league franchises controlled by major-league clubs or their owners. Branch Rickey's ultimate vision of a true farm system was beginning to fall into place. It was also beginning to pay off. In 1929 the Cardinals bought pitcher Jesse Haines for $10,000. It was a good deal; Haines went on to win 210 games for St. Louis over a 19-year, Hall-of-Fame career. Haines was a milestone, however, because he was the last major player purchased by Rickey's Cardinals. The St. Louis dynasty that defeated Babe Ruth's Yankees in 1926 and played in three more World Series between 1928 and 1934, culminating in the infamous "Gas House Gang" club of the mid-1930s, was 99 percent home-grown by Rickey's farm system.

Today, thanks to the success of Branch Rickey and his Cardinals, every major-league baseball club has a farm system and the minor leagues are no longer independent; they serve more or less as schools for major-league prospects. In the 1920s, however, Rickey's farm system was a very controversial idea. Most baseball people, Commissioner Landis included, felt that independent minor leagues were essential to the health of the baseball business. Landis further saw Rickey's farm system as a way to evade the option rules, which limited how many players a club could use at any one time, by stockpiling players unfairly and holding them down in the minors for the convenience of the big-league club.

Fortunately for Rickey, his idea was not exactly illegal under baseball law. The 1903 National Agreement had outlawed under-the-table arrangements between major- and minor-league clubs but not outright ownership of one by the other. In the mid-1910s Ban Johnson's National Commission tried to outlaw such dual ownership but, distracted by the Federal League War and the power struggles of 1918–20, never enforced the rule. The new 1921 National Agreement negotiated by Landis failed to include an anti-farm system provision, but only because owners like Pittsburgh's Barney Dreyfuss and Detroit's Frank Navin assured Landis that Rickey's idea was impractical and would never fly. By the late 1920s, Landis realized that Dreyfuss and Navin were wrong, but it was too late; in fact, both the Tigers and Pirates were taking steps to set up farm systems of their own.

It was too late for Landis to stop other owners from emulating Rickey, but characteristically, he was stubborn enough to try. He could not rule farm systems illegal, but he resolved to watch Rickey's and the other owners' every move in case they used the new system to abuse players' rights. In 1921 he had freed four minor-leaguers from their contracts and fined three major-league clubs for abusing the option rules. In 1928 Landis publicly attacked major-league ownership of minor-league clubs, comparing it to an act of "rape." Branch Rickey defended himself by claiming, with some justification, that major-league investment was saving many minor leagues. When he talked about the farm system, however, Rickey sounded more like a Wall Street corporate raider or a military strategist than a philanthropist:

> *I believe the farm system is definitely right, first on the ground of efficiency in operation; second on its in-bred economy; and third, on the marvelous promotional programs that you can*

Commissioner Landis throws out the opening pitch at a major-league game. Landis opposed the efforts of Branch Rickey to establish a farm system for the St. Louis Cardinals.

get from it from finding and developing raw material. It is the only promotional program I can think of that has in it the wide extension of interest in organized baseball in developing young talent. It is high class. It is a frontal attack. It is wide open, progressive, efficient, and healthy.[1]

Landis ranted, kicked, and screamed against the farm system all the way into the early 1940s. He twice ordered the release of nearly 100 minor-leaguers each from the Detroit and St. Louis organizations. But by then the independent minors Landis was fighting for no longer existed; in 1940 the Cardinals alone controlled 33 minor-league clubs and had supplied several dozen players to other big-league teams. Branch Rickey had shown the way, and the rest of baseball was lining up to follow. As powerful as he was, Kenesaw Mountain Landis could not turn back the future. As for Rickey, his work was far from complete. He had other plans that would rock the baseball boat even harder in the coming decades.

THE YEAR: 1928

In 1928 the Yankees came down from the higher league they seemed to have been playing in, in 1927, and were surprised to find themselves in a dogfight for the pennant. The Bronx Bombers started out of the gate strong and finished with a 101–53 record, but Connie Mack's resurgent Athletics put on a 25–8 stretch in July and—carried by slugger Al Simmons, who batted .351, and ace pitcher Lefty Grove, who was first in the AL in wins with 24, first in strikeouts with 183, and third in ERA at 2.58—nipped at the Yankees' heels through August before finally pulling even in September. The 1928 A's were a talented blend of youth and age, including the up-and-coming Simmons, home-run man Jimmie "The Beast" Foxx, and MVP catcher Mickey Cochrane; plus dead-ball veterans Cobb, who hit .323, Tris Speaker, and Eddie Collins—all making one last run at a final career pennant. The Philadelphia line-up was rounded out by outfielder Bing Miller, who was fifth in batting at .329, and lead-off man Max Bishop, who drew 97 walks and scored 104 runs. Mack's versatile pitching staff was made up of 28-year-old Lefty Grove, 17–12 Rube Walberg, 13–5 Eddie Rommel, and old men Jack Quinn, who went 18–7 at the age of 44, and Howard Ehmke. The A's' and Yanks' showdown came at a September 9 double-header at Yankee Stadium, which was attended by a record crowd of 85, 264; the Yankees swept, 3-0 and 7-3, and went on to clinch the AL flag less than two weeks later. Philadelphia won 98 games but finished 2½ games out.

The Yankees' pitching staff slumped in 1928; only Pipgras and Hoyt won over 20 games, and only Pennock made the ERA leader board. The hitters, however, picked up the slack. They once again led the league in runs, with 894, and home runs, with 133, 44 more than the nearest competitor. Ruth and Gehrig were first and second in home runs with 54 and 27, runs with 163 and 139, and slugging at .709 and 648; they tied for the league lead in RBIs with 142.

Washington's Goose Goslin won his only career batting title at .379, just beating out St. Louis's Heinie Manush, who hit .378 with 20 triples, 108 RBIs, and a league-leading 47 doubles.

The NL race was another close battle, as the 95–59 Cardinals outlasted a game Giants team that won 25 games in September only to come up two games short at 93–61. The Cardinals' Jim Bottomley led the NL in triples with 20; he tied the Cubs' Hack Wilson for the home-run title with 31. The St. Louis line-up was fortified by young outfielders Chick Hafey, who hit .337 and belted 46 doubles and 27 homers; and Taylor Douthit, who drew 84 walks and scored 111 runs. The Giants matched the Cardinals' total of 807 runs on the strength of Bill Terry's .326 average and 101 RBIs; Fred Lindstrom's .358 mark and 39 doubles; and the 19-year-old Mel Ott's .322 average and team-leading 18 home runs.

*Philadelphia A's owner and manager Connie Mack
and his ace pitcher Lefty Grove pose before their
September 9, 1928, doubleheader with the
New York Yankees. The Yankees swept the
twin-bill, which helped them clinch the
pennant by 2½ games over the A's.*

Playing for his third team in three seasons, Boston's irascible Rogers Hornsby led the league in hitting at .387, on-base average at .498 , and slugging at .632. Pittsburgh's Burleigh Grimes and New York's Larry Benton tied for the lead in wins with 25 and Dazzy Vance took the ERA title at 2.09.

The Yankees repeated their dominating performance of the year before as they swept the 1928 series, four games to none. New York hitters scored 27 runs, 17 more than their pitchers allowed, and out-homered the Cardinals nine to one. To make their revenge for 1926 complete, the Yanks defeated Pete Alexander 9-3 in his only start; he recorded an ugly series ERA of 19.80.

CHAPTER NINE

In the Shadow of the Babe: Hall of Famers from the 1920s

Ballplayers from the 1920s are more than fairly represented in the baseball Hall of Fame in Cooperstown. By a rough count, 33 out of the 166 major leaguers elected to the Hall, or almost 20 percent, are men who played at least half of their careers between 1920 and 1929. There is probably a good explanation for this: people tend to overrate players that they saw or heard about as children or young fans. As the years pass, those players acquire a magical patina that today's superstars, no matter how skilled, can never match. When the Hall of Fame was opened in 1939, the writers and committees who voted on the first couple of dozen players to be enshrined naturally favored the heroes of the previous generation.

Regardless of whether they were done right by baseball posterity, however, most of the 33 Hall of Famers from the 1920s have faded from the memory of today's fans. Many have been lost in the vast shadow cast by Babe Ruth, Lou Gehrig, and the rest of the New York Yankees—the most dominant player and one of the most dominant teams not only of the 1920s, but of all time. Even though you would never know it from some baseball history books, there were lots of great players from the 1920s who did not wear pinstripes. An excellent fantasy all-star team could be made entirely of non-Yankee Hall of Famers from that decade. The team might well look something like this:

Charles "Gabby" Hartnett, catcher. One of the most durable catchers of the pre-World War II era, Hartnett was the National League's answer to Mickey Cochrane and later, Bill Dickey. Called the "Perfect Catcher" by manager Joe McCarthy, the shy, soft-spoken Hartnett anchored the Chicago Cubs' defense from 1922 to 1940. A respected handler of pitchers and the possessor of a magnificent throwing arm, from 1924 through 1937 he caught over 100 games every year but two and retired with the career record for most games caught, 1,790. He was a solid hitter, too, averaging .297 in his 20 years in the majors and developing in mid-career into a middle-of-the-order power hitter. He hit 24 home runs in 1925 and 37 in 1930; with 236 career homers he remained baseball's all-time top home-run-hitting catcher until the arrival of Roy Campanella and Yogi Berra in the 1950s.

After seven brilliant seasons with a non-contender, Hartnett suffered a career-threatening arm injury and played only 25 games in 1929, the year the Cubs won their first NL pennant since 1918. He came back strong, however, in 1930 to hit .339 with 37 home runs and 122 RBIs; in 1935 Hartnett batted .344, won the MVP, and led the Cubs to their third World Series appearance of the decade. The finest single day of his career came on September 28, 1938, in a game against Pittsburgh at Wrigley Field. The Cubs and Pirates were battling for the pennant, and player/manager Hartnett had brought his club to within a half-game of first place. With the sun setting, the score tied, the count 0-2, and two out in the bottom of the ninth, Hartnett drove his famous "Homer in the Gloamin' " out of the park; three days later the Cubs clinched the NL flag. As a manager in the late 1930s, Hartnett became one of the few in baseball to risk Commissioner Landis's wrath by advocating the signing of African-Americans to major-league contracts.

George Sisler, first base. You could call George Sisler a Lou Gehrig with speed or a Ty Cobb with power; either way Sisler was one of baseball's greatest all-around offensive forces. The problem is that he had only half of a great career; in 1923, at the age of 28, he missed the entire season with an eye infection. After that, he was merely very good.

Like Babe Ruth, Sisler came up as an excellent left-handed pitcher. After a little more than one season, however, the St. Louis Browns moved him to first base, where he flashed a solid gold glove, and let him hit. From 1917 on, he batted .353, .341, .352, .407, .371, and .420. In 1920, he had one of the greatest baseball seasons in any era. He played every inning of every Browns game, won the batting title at .407, hit 42 doubles, 18 triples, and 8 homers; his 257 hits remain an all-time major-league record. In 1922 Sisler batted .420 and put together an AL-record 41-game hit streak; this was the record broken by Joe DiMaggio in 1941.

An amazing fielder, Sisler was famous for turning doubles into outs and squeeze bunts into double plays; he had speed, too, leading the AL in stolen bases in 1918, 1921, 1922, and 1927. Even though Sisler was never the same after his return from eye problems in 1923, he still batted over .300 seven times, including a season in 1924 when he hit .345 with 15 triples, 12 homers, and 105 RBIs. He hit .309 in his last year in the big leagues and retired with a career .340 batting average.

Rogers Hornsby, second base. The greatest right-handed hitter in major-league history, Rogers Hornsby had a career that was covered in glory, honors, and awards. The odd thing was, they came with five different major-league clubs. An unpleasant, inconsiderate, and outspoken man with a fierce contempt for authority, Hornsby could outwear his welcome and bat .400 at the same time; he was traded in his prime more than any other player of his class.

Known as the "Rajah," Hornsby was traded after some of greatest batting seasons in history. Coming up with the St. Louis Cardinals as a shortstop in 1916, he developed into a mediocre defensive second baseman with a deadly bat. Like many great hitters for average, Hornsby held a set of quirky personal beliefs; he was convinced, for example, that reading, watching movies, drinking coffee, and drinking alcohol were all bad for the batting eye. It is not known what he did to pass the time away from the baseball field. A .300-hitter with doubles power throughout the 1910s, he blossomed into a home-run threat with the advent of Babe Ruth and the home-run revolution in 1920. After hitting .370 with 44 doubles and 20 triples and 94 RBIs in 1920, a great dead-ball type season, Hornsby swatted 21 home runs, hit .397, and led the league in runs, hits, doubles, triples, and RBIs the following year.

Hornsby's next four seasons stand up to any set of four consecutive seasons by one player in history: he collected 250, 163, 227, and 203 hits; 46, 32, 43, and 41 doubles; 14, 10, 14, and 10 triples; 42, 17, 25, and 39 home runs; 152, 83, 94, and 143 RBIs. As for average, Hornsby batted an unthinkable .401, .384, .424, and .403.

A two-time Triple-Crown winner and two-time MVP, Hornsby retired with 532 doubles, 298 homers, and a .358 lifetime batting average. As a player/manager Hornsby took Branch Rickey's place in the dugout and

Most baseball authorities consider Rogers Hornsby, pictured here in 1921 when he played for the St. Louis Cardinals, as the greatest right-handed hitter in major-league history.

led the Cardinals to their first NL pennant in 1926. After quarreling with the Cards over money, in 1927 Hornsby was traded to the Giants, where John McGraw and Charles Stoneham soon had their fill of his insubordination and corrosive clubhouse presence; in 1928 the Giants sent him to the Boston Braves for a pair of ordinary players. The following year Hornsby made it four teams in four years when Chicago Cubs president William Veeck, Sr., landed him for five no-name players and cash. He was released by Chicago after batting .331 with 16 homers and 90 RBIs, picked up by the Cardinals, and released again the following year. When Bill Veeck, Jr., signed him for the St. Louis Browns in 1933, he got a note from his mother that read: "What makes you think you're smarter than your daddy was?"

Even though he was almost universally disliked, the cold and demanding Hornsby had a long post-playing career as a minor-league manager and major-league coach and scout; he was the hitting coach on the 1962 original New York Mets. Like many stars-turned-coaches or managers, Hornsby seemed unable to understand why he could not teach less talented players to hit the way he did. His 1962 autobiography was fittingly titled: *My War with Baseball*.

THE YEAR: 1929

Connie Mack brought his Philadelphia A's back to first place in 1929 after a 15-year pennant drought. It was a long, difficult climb; after finishing dead last seven years in a row after 1915, the team finished seventh in 1922, sixth in 1923, fifth in 1924, third in 1925 and 1926, and second in 1927 and 1928. Mack built his team on young sluggers Al Simmons and Jimmie Foxx; the two were third and fourth in the AL in home runs,

142

with totals of 34 and 33, behind only Ruth at 46 and Gehrig at 35. From the minor-league Baltimore Orioles, Babe Ruth's former club, Mack purchased Foxx, second baseman Max Bishop, back-up infielder Jimmy Dykes, and the heart of his pitching staff: 29-year old Lefty Grove, who won the ERA title at 2.81, and righty George Earnshaw, who went 24–8 to lead the AL in wins. The A's recorded the AL's best ERA at 3.44; they were the only staff under 4.00.

The AL race was over early, as Mack's 104–46 "White Elephants" trampled the opposition; at 18 games out, New York was the only team within two dozen games of the lead. Ruth and Gehrig had their usual great years, but Bob Meusel slumped to .261 with only ten home runs; the Yankees got little offense out of Leo Durocher at short or Gene Robertson at third. Only one Yankees starting pitcher, Tom Zachary, turned in an ERA below 4.00. Led by Charlie Gehringer, who scored an AL-high 131 runs and 19 triples, sixth-place Detroit had the AL's leading offense with 926 runs; Cleveland first baseman Lew Fonseca took the batting title at .369.

At 98–54 Chicago finished first in the NL for the first time since 1918; Pittsburgh came in second, 10½ games back. The Cubs boasted the fearsomest right-handed hitting attack of all time, as left fielder Riggs Stephenson batted .362; center fielder Hack Wilson hit .345; and right fielder Kiki Cuyler hit .360. This trio combined for 71 homers, 337 runs, and 271 RBIs. The infield featured a double play combination of shortstop Woody English and perennial MVP and trade bait Rogers Hornsby, who was third in the NL in batting at .380, third in home runs with 39, first in runs with 156, and third in RBIs with 149. Pat Malone led the Cubs and the NL in wins with 22, Charlie Root was second with 19, and Root and Malone were third and fourth in ERA at 3.47 and

3.57; starter/reliever Guy Bush won 18 and appeared in an NL-high 50 games. Playing in tiny Baker Bowl, the fifth-place Phillies lit up the scoreboard. MVP runner-up Lefty O'Doul led the NL in hitting at .398, swatted 32 homers, and knocked out 254 hits, still the NL record, and Chuck Klein led in home runs with 43 and batted .356. Philadelphia pitchers, however, undid their work by allowing an incredible 1,032 runs.

The 1929 World Series opened with one of the gutsiest gambles in series history, when Connie Mack sent out washed-up reliever Howard Ehmke to face the Cubs' right-handed wrecking crew in game one; left-handed 18-game winner Walberg and future Hall of Famer Lefty Grove were relegated to the bullpen and worked only a combined 12⅔ innings in the series. The gamble paid off handsomely, as Ehmke struck out 13 with his slow stuff and recorded a 3-1 win. Righties George Earnshaw and Eddie Rommel also got the best of Chicago as Philadelphia won the series, four games to one. A great moment came in game four, when the A's overcame an 8-0 deficit with a wacky ten-run seventh that included four Cubs pitchers and two balls lost in the sun by Hack Wilson. This is still the biggest-scoring inning in World Series history.

Joe Sewell, shortstop. Thrown into the pressure-cooker in 1920, when he was brought up from the minors to replace the dead Ray Chapman in a three-team dogfight for the AL pennant, Cleveland's Joe Sewell responded by hitting .329 and fielding his position flawlessly. He soon developed into the personification of the term "steady." A graceful fielder, Sewell played a then-record streak of 1,103 straight games for the Indians between 1922 and 1930. He could be an offensive force as well; although he lacked home-run punch, Sewell regularly hit around 40 doubles and batted .312 lifetime; twice he drove in 100 runs.

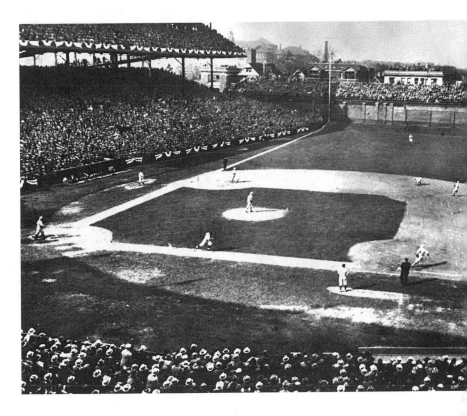

At Chicago's Wrigley Field, A's lead-off hitter Max Bishop grounds out in the first game of the 1929 World Series. Mack's Philadelphia squad defeated the Cubs four games to one to clinch the series.

What leaps off Sewell's page in the baseball encyclopedia, however, is his strikeout column. Sewell used a huge 40-ounce bat and a short swing; this combined with a phenomenal batting eye made him the hardest man in major-league history to strike out. While drawing 844 lifetime walks, he whiffed a total of only 114 times in 7,132 games over 14 years. Three times he

Cleveland shortstop Joe Sewell was the hardest man to strike out in major-league history.

played an entire season with fewer than four strikeouts. His career walk-to-strikeout ratio of better than 7:1 will never be approached by another major-league hitter.

Pie Traynor, third base. The strange thing about Traynor, who played 17 years with the Pittsburgh Pirates, is that even though he was considered the best third baseman in baseball history for almost 30 years, modern fans know almost nothing about him. Part of the reason may be that he was overrated; another part of the reason is that modern fans are living in an age of great third basemen. The fact is that in the past three decades, we have been spoiled by being treated to all-time greats like Brooks Robinson, Mike Schmidt, Graig Nettles, Ron Santo, and George Brett—most of them better fielders than Traynor and every one of them a far better hitter.

In his time, however, Traynor was certainly one of the best. While no power threat by the standards of the 1920s, Traynor swung a good bat, hitting over .300 ten times and retiring with a gaudy .320 lifetime average; an excellent contact hitter batting in a strong line-up, he drove in 100 runs or more seven times. His finest season at the plate came when his team needed it most, in the 1925 pennant race; Traynor batted .320, scored 144 runs, and drove in 106 during the regular season and hit .346 with two triples and a home run (off Walter Johnson) in the series. Fielding was what Traynor was paid for. He was durable, dependable, and showed terrific range. He led the NL in put outs at third base a record seven times and led the league in double plays every year from 1924 through 1927.

Goose Goslin, left field. Goose Goslin was the original "Mr. October." Like modern slugger Reggie Jackson, Goslin was a good-hit, no-field outfielder; he batted left with good power. Playing 18 years in the AL for Washington, St. Louis, and Detroit, he was a steady RBI-man, driving in 100 runs 11 times in the middle 13 years of his career. In a typical season, Goslin hit 36 doubles, 15 triples, and 20 homers. A .316 lifetime hitter, he batted over .330 five times, won the 1928 batting title at .379, and finished his career with 2,735 hits.

It was in the World Series, however, that Goslin's star shined brightest. With the Senators, he swatted three home runs each in the World Series of 1924 and 1925. With Detroit in 1934, Goslin drove in the winning run in game two; the following year he had the biggest hit of the series, beating the Cubs with a game-winning single in the bottom of the ninth of the final game.

Al Simmons, center field. Born Aloys Szymanski in the Polish section of Milwaukee, Wisconsin, Simmons was famous for the unorthodox batting style that earned him the nickname "Bucketfoot Al." Standing far from the plate, the right-handed Simmons would open up early and drag his long bat through the strike zone. Although this has long been considered a classic batting flaw, Simmons's first manager Connie Mack refused to let anyone change his swing. The reason was simple: Simmons's swing got results.

Al Simmons played as hard—and hit the ball as hard—as anyone in baseball in the 1920s. He ran the bases aggressively but intelligently, played a solid center field, and sprayed line drives all over the park. A .337 lifetime hitter, mostly with Philadelphia, Simmons collected over 200 hits six times, including a near-record 253 in 1925; he batted over .330 nine times, winning back-to-back batting titles in 1930 and 1931 at .381 and .390, respectively. He regularly hit over 40 doubles and three times hit 30 or more homers.

Like Goose Goslin, Simmons often saved his best for the World Series. He hit six home runs in only 19 career series games. He also played a key role in the most famous inning in Philadelphia Athletics' history, the seventh inning of the fourth game of the 1929 series against the Chicago Cubs. With his team down 8-0 entering the inning, Simmons lead off the inning with a

Slugger Al Simmons, a lifetime .337 hitter,
was one of the greatest players of the 1920s.

homer. The score was 8-7 by the time Simmons came to the plate for the second time in the inning; he singled and the A's added two more runs to win the biggest come-from-behind victory in World Series history.

Harry Heilmann, right field. Like Pie Traynor, Harry Heilmann is largely forgotten by today's fans. There are reasons for this, chiefly that he had little home-run power and never appeared in a postseason game. But Heilmann could hit. A line-drive, high-average hitter in the tradition of his manager and mentor, Ty Cobb, Heilmann produced seven or eight Cobb-like seasons after the rules changes of 1920 and 1921. A .280 to .290 hitter before the home-run explosion, he batted a league-leading .394 with 237 hits and 139 RBIs in 1921. After that, Heilmann became a perennial 100-run and 100-RBI man; he routinely hit around 40 doubles, 10 or 12 triples, and 15 or so homers. He also put together a string of batting titles, hitting a stratospheric .403 in 1923, .393 in 1925, and .398 in 1927. Harry Heilmann developed arthritis and played only 15 games after the 1930 season, when he was 35. He retired in 1932 with a .342 career batting average and 2,660 hits.

Grover Cleveland "Pete" Alexander, starting pitcher. A classic dead-ball era control pitcher when he came up to the majors with the Philadelphia Phillies in 1911, Alexander pitched for so long that he really had two careers: one from 1911 to 1920; another from 1921 to his retirement in 1930. The two halves of Alexander's career add up to 373 wins—tied for third on the all-time list with Christy Mathewson—and 208 losses, with a 2.56 ERA over 20 years.

In the first phase of his career, Alexander was as dominant as a Mathewson or a Cy Young. Thanks to an easy pitching motion, a deceptive sinker, and pinpoint control, he regularly pitched over 350 innings; won 25 to 30 games; lost around 10; recorded an ERA in the 1.00s; and led the league in both strikeouts and ERA—all this in tiny, hitter-friendly Baker Bowl. As one NL hitter said of Alexander's stuff: "Once [the pitches] showed you what they were going to do and where they were going to do it, they were somewhere else."

Alexander adjusted beautifully to the changes that brought the home-run revolution of 1920 and 1921, which ended many pitching careers. He never again threw 350 innings, led the league in strikeouts, or won an ERA title; all he did was keep on winning. Instead of going 30–12, the 1920s version of Pete Alexander went 15–11 or 16–13; and he did it season in and season out. Pitching mostly for the Chicago Cubs and the St. Louis Cardinals in the home-run era, Alexander produced nine winning seasons in a row and added 140 victories to his career total.

Pete Alexander battled more than opposing line-ups during his two decades in the majors; he also struggled with a terrible drinking problem compounded by epilepsy. In photographs of the inevitably scowling Alexander, you can read the pain and worry in his face. Ex-teammate Bill Hallahan described the unhappy pitcher as "a loner. He would go off by himself and do what he did, which I suppose was drink." Baseball history is full of hard-drinking pitchers who manage to keep their careers going for years before the alcohol catches up with them, but Pete Alexander lasted longer than most. He was 43 when he finally burned out as a major-league pitcher. He went on to become a some-what pathetic character, living off his name or hand-outs from old friends; Alexander died in 1950 at the age of 64.

The high point of Alexander's career came in the seventh game of the 1926 World Series, when he came out of the bullpen to face Yankees slugger Tony Lazzeri with the bases loaded, two out, and game and the series on the line. He was coming into his third game in six days; the day before he had thrown a complete-game

Pitcher Grover Cleveland "Pete" Alexander, the hero of the 1926 World Series, had 373 career wins.

10-2 victory. Still, he had enough left in his 39-year-old right arm to strike out Lazzeri on four low fastballs; he then went on to pitch two more scoreless innings to win the series.

* * * * *

This fantasy all-star team of forgotten non-Yankee Hall-of-Famers from the 1920s would stack up well against the best of most decades in baseball history. It might be a little short in the pitching and power departments, but it has a terrific defense, particularly in the infield; and the team as a whole would probably bat around .340. But could it beat the 1927 New York Yankees of Ruth, Gehrig, Lazzeri, Hoyt, Meusel, and Combs? That is hard to say. One thing is certain, however—not many baseball fans of the 1920s would have bet on it.

Source Notes

CHAPTER ONE
1. J. G. Taylor Spink, *Judge Landis and 25 Years of Baseball* (New York: Crowell, 1947), p. 45.

CHAPTER TWO
1. Dave Anderson, *Pennant Races* (New York: Doubleday, 1994), p. 61.
2. Spink, p. 65.

CHAPTER THREE
1. Eliot Asinof, *Eight Men Out* (New York: Holt, Rinehart and Winston, 1963), p. 267.
2. Eugene Murdock, *Ban Johnson: Czar of Baseball* (Westport, CT: Greenwood Press, 1982), p. 211.

CHAPTER FOUR
1. William Curran, *Big Sticks* (New York: HarperCollins, 1990), pp. 81–82.
2. Marshall Smelser, *The Life That Ruth Built* (Lincoln, NE: Univ. of Nebraska Press, 1975), p. 170.

3. Jonathan Yardley in *The Armchair Book of Baseball,* John Thorn, ed. (New York: Scribner's, 1985), p. 385.

CHAPTER FIVE
1. Fred Lieb, *Baseball As I Have Known It* (New York: Grossett and Dunlap, 1977), p. 165.
2. John Tullius, *I'd Rather Be a Yankee* (New York: Macmillan, 1986), p. 47.

CHAPTER SEVEN
1. Robert Creamer, *Babe* (New York: Penguin, 1983), pp. 302–03.
2. John Tullius, *I'd Rather Be a Yankee* (New York: Macmillan, 1986), p. 92.
3. Lawrence Ritter and Mark Rucker, *The Babe: A Life in Pictures* (New York: Ticknor and Fields, 1988), p. 139.
4. Lee Allen, *100 Years of Baseball* (New York: Bartholomew House, 1950), p. 205.

CHAPTER EIGHT
1. John Monteleone, ed., *Branch Rickey's Little Blue Book* (New York: Macmillan, 1995), p. 63.

Bibliography

Alexander, Charles. *John McGraw.* New York: Viking, 1988.

Allen, Lee. *100 Years of Baseball.* New York: Bartholomew House, 1950.

———. *The American League Story.* New York: Hill and Wang, 1962.

———. *The National League Story.* New York: Hill and Wang, 1961.

Axelson, G. W. *Commy.* Chicago: Reilly and Lee, 1919.

Barrow, Ed. *My 50 Years in Baseball.* New York: Coward-McCann, 1951.

Creamer, Robert. *The Babe.* New York: Penguin, 1983.

Curran, William. *Big Sticks.* New York: HarperCollins, 1990.

Gershman, Michael. *Diamonds: The Evolution of the Ballpark.* Boston: Houghton Mifflin, 1993.

Koppett, Leonard. *The Man in the Dugout.* New York: Crown, 1993.

James, Bill: *The Bill James Historical Baseball Abstract.* New York: Villard, 1988.

Lieb, Fred. *Baseball As I Have Known It.* New York: Grosset and Dunlap, 1977.

———. *The Story of the World Series.* New York: Putnam, 1965.

Murdock, Eugene. *Ban Johnson, Czar of Baseball.* Westport, CT: Greenwood, 1982.

Peterson, Robert. *Only the Ball was White.* New York: McGraw-Hill, 1970.

Quigley, Martin. *The Crooked Pitch.* Chapel Hill: Algonquin, 1984.

Reichler, Joseph, ed. *The Baseball Encyclopedia.* New York: MacMillan, 1988.

Ritter, Lawrence: *The Glory of Their Times.* New York: Morrow, 1984.

Seymour, Harold. *Baseball:The Golden Age.* New York: Oxford Univ. Press, 1971.

Smelser, Marshall. *The Life that Ruth Built.* Lincoln: Univ. of Nebraska Press, 1975.

Spink, J. G. Taylor. *Judge Landis and 25 Years of Baseball.* New York: Crowell, 1947.

Thorn, John, and Pete Palmer, eds. *Total Baseball,* 3rd ed. New York: HarperCollins, 1993.

Index

DATE DUE
